THE STORY OF

FOULRIDGE

BY FAY OLDLAND

PUBLISHED BY  NOYNA PUBLISHING

Dedication

To the memory of
Geoffrey Richard Sutton M.B.E
1934-2007
the catalyst for making the book a reality

First published in 1990 by Pendle Heritage Centre.

This revised, second edition published in 2010
by Noyna Publishing, Village Hall, Parkinson Street, Foulridge, Colne,
Lancashire BB8 7PS.

© Fay Oldland, 1990, 2010

All images © Robert Oldland, 1990, 2010
unless otherwise acknowledged

All efforts have been made to trace copyright holders, but if any have been
inadvertently omitted, please contact the publisher.

ISBN: 978-0-9565366-0-0

Design and illustration by John Westwell

Printed and bound by Peter Scott Printers Ltd, Burnley

Cover photograph by Andrew Wilson

CONTENTS

ACKNOWLEDGEMENTS

I would like to express my sincere thanks to the many people who have helped in the research and publication. I remain indebted to Dennis Green, the original instigator of the book, and to the mentors of the first edition – Peter Wightman, Doreen Crowther, Allen Exley, Roland Halstead and Nellie Dalby – all of whom generously gave time and encouragement over a period of years discussing ideas and information.

I am grateful to Foulridge Parish Council and Clerks, both past and present, for providing access to Parish records and consistent support of village history projects. The Council's commitment to having the village's history recorded for future generations is demonstrated by the setting up of its own publishing company 'Noyna Publishing' to facilitate publication.

I would particularly like to thank Mildred Wightman for her carefully considered initial editing of the text for this revised edition, to Andrew Wilson for his detective work and proof reading of the final script, and to Christine Bradley and the staff at Colne Library for whom, as always, nothing seemed too much trouble.

I wish to thank the owners of properties for their enthusiastic co-operation, and to the many individuals who have helped in various ways by providing documents, photographs and verifying information. They include Bill Badgery, John Bank, Robert & Christine Bank, Marshal Brown, Iain Bulcock, Graham Cannon, Mr G L Clarke, Donald Croasdale, David Duckworth, Helen Eddy, William Fishwick, Mildred Fletcher, Ted Fort, Stanley Graham, Hilary Gregg, John Hartley, Mary Hook, Jean Kneller, Dennis Mendoros, Raymond Mitchell, Gordon Moorhouse, Jean Rigg, June Steele, and Hazel Wilkinson. I apologize for any inadvertent omissions.

I would like to acknowledge Charles Green, David Ingham, Rob Oldland, Pendle Movie Makers, Thomas Robinson, Peter Wightman, and Andrew Wilson for photography. I would also like to thank Jean Kneller, Malcolm Waterworth, and Malcolm Whalley for the loan of photographic material, Mrs Diana Parker for permission to reproduce the Browsholme Hall portraits, and John Westwell for allowing use of illustrations produced for the first edition.

Special thanks are due to my husband, Rob, for his invaluable and unfailing support, not only for his photography but also his constructive advice and being my sounding board.

Finally, my heartfelt thanks go to Geoffrey Sutton's family, the Fort Foundation and Foulridge Parish Council for their wholehearted support and sponsorship, and without whom this book would not have been published. As well as generously defraying the cost of printing, they have agreed that the proceeds of book sales should be donated to village organizations and community projects administered by the Parish Council.

Fay Oldland
April 2010

FOREWORD

It was a great privilege to be invited to read, and write a foreword to this remarkable history of Foulridge – a journey through time from the Middle Ages to the present day.

I have lived in Foulridge for 53 years, and Geoffrey and I always felt fortunate to be part of a very special village.

Thank you Fay, and all others involved in the publication of this fascinating book. May it give much pleasure to everyone who reads it.

Ruth Sutton
March 2010

INTRODUCTION

The village of Foulridge (pronounced 'foalridge') lies about 1½ miles to the north of Colne in North East Lancashire. For centuries the village bordered the old West Riding of Yorkshire but, since 1974 Local Government Reorganization, along with its Craven neighbours, Foulridge became part of the Borough of Pendle, so named after the Borough's best known feature and landmark – Pendle Hill.

Foulridge today has an area of 1600 acres. Formerly it was half as large again, and consisted of two separate parts. One, comprising Barnside, Monkroyd and Laneshawbridge, was known as **Foulridge Detached** as it was completely surrounded by Colne. In 1935 it officially became part of Colne.

The centre of Foulridge occupies a valley running in a north/south direction. To the east Noyna Hill rises to a height of about 980' above sea level, while to the west 786' is reached at Pasture Head. It has a typical mid-Pennine landscape – moors and hills interspersed with drystone walls and small valleys. The soil is sand and loam, overlying Millstone Grit. The land is mostly used for pasture. Low lying parts of the village were once covered by extensive marshes as is reflected by names such as Reedymoor and Moss House. In the depression between Foulridge and Salterforth (known as 'the Bottoms') are remnants of former marshlands which were drained in the early 19th century.

Almost all land is over 500'. The Leeds & Liverpool Canal reaches its summit level as it passes through the village which is the reason for the principal compensation reservoirs for the canal being constructed in the neighbourhood.

The hills on the skyline represent the watershed of the Pennines. No rivers run directly through the village, a factor which contributed to the village's late transition from hand to power loom. There are, however, a number of small streams. One ran along the valley and joined Wanless Beck at the bottom of Slipper Hill. Up to this point the stream was called King's Beck and this drained down from Great Edge, a small tributary called Bar Beck running down off Noyna. These streams run down into Pendle Water, then into the Calder and eventually join the Ribble and flow into the Irish Sea. On the northern side of Standing Stone Lane, becks rising on the side of White Moor run into Whitemoor Reservoir and out of it as County Brook. This flows into the Foulridge valley bottoms and joins Lancashire Ghyll from Kelbrook Moor via the New Cut to become Earby Beck and ultimately join the Aire, Ouse, and Trent to form the mighty Humber.

The **Pennine watershed** runs along the backbone of northern England and separates the headwaters of those rivers which flow into the Irish Sea from those which flow into the North Sea. It is interesting to reflect that within a matter of

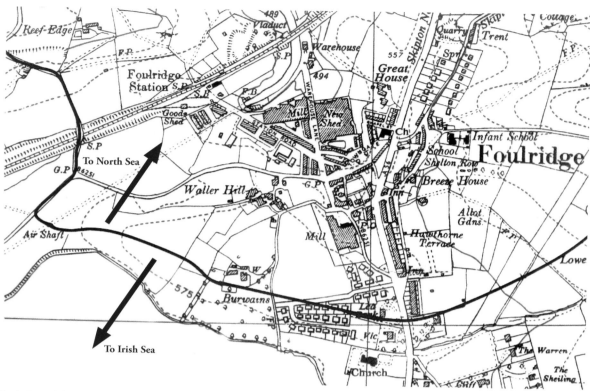

Foulridge and the Pennine Watershed.

a few hundred yards, and depending on the vagaries of the wind, any rain falling in Foulridge could either find its way to the Irish Sea on the west coast or to the North Sea on the east.

The population of the village remained fairly steady throughout the 1900s at around the 1,350 mark, but reached a peak of 1,734 in 2001 occupying 731 households. The population of the mid-19th century consisted chiefly of weavers, farmers and watermen virtually all of whom worked in the village. Improved roads and increased mobility have led to the village becoming largely residential in recent years.

The canal no longer provides the main form of goods transport and work, but leisure is becoming increasingly important and more and more people are enjoying a wide variety of leisure pursuits in and around the village – canal cruising, sailing, walking and fishing to name a few.

Chapter 1

EARLY HISTORY

The discovery of a Bronze Age axe head near Hobstones in the 1980s suggests the presence of early man in Foulridge by about 2,000 B.C., and the name 'Burwains' suggests a possible burial dating to this period which has yet to be discovered.

The earliest evidence of settlement in the village is the celtic walling at the foot of Noyna left by the Brigantes, a tribe of Ancient Britons who occupied this area during the Iron Age. The Roman occupation left few marks in the hostile Pennines. Their military road from Ribchester to York passed within a few miles north of Foulridge and the district may have seen some minor rebellion as well as sporadic clashes with the native Celts.

The withdrawal of the Romans led to invasion by successive tribes from Europe. The first to arrive in the Pendle district were the Angles in the 7th century. The fact that Foulridge derives its name from the Anglo-Saxon words for foal and ridge suggests that it was established by the Angles and took its name from the ridge where they grazed their foals (possibly Pasture Head).

Placename evidence indicates that Vikings had settled on the outskirts of the village by the 9th century, generally occupying upland areas (like the lands they had left). Their brooks were *'becks'*, their valleys *'gills'*, and tracks *'gates'* – all common elements in Foulridge names. The Norsemen were herdsmen and used remote hillsides for summer grazing. Barnside, from the Old Norse for 'Biorn's mountain pasture' was such a shieling.

Bronze Age axe head found near Hobstones in 1986 by D J Cunliffe of Colne.

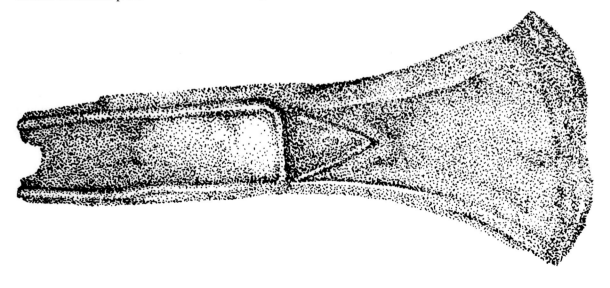

The mixture of both Old English and Norse place names suggests that the Angles and Norsemen coexisted locally in tiny hamlets at a distance from one another. Gradually more Norsemen infiltrated the district as the whole of North Lancashire became part of the Danelaw, ruled by the Viking Kingdom of Northumbria. After the Battle of Brunanburgh, however, many Norsemen were driven northwards and the area described as being *'between the Ribble and the Mersey'* became part of the Anglo Saxon kingdom, and organised in divisions called Hundreds. Foulridge became part of the **Hundred of Blackburn**, which covered an area stretching from Foulridge to Accrington, and from Cliviger to Chatburn.

Chapter 2

THE MEDIEVAL MANOR

Other than the occasional archaeological find and place name evidence, little is known about life in the village before the Middle Ages when written records begin. References to the village's name, along with those of Accornley, Barnside and Monkroyd go back to the 1200s.

Neither Colne nor Foulridge are mentioned in the **Domesday Book** of 1086 which only devoted one and a half pages to the entire region *'inter Ripam et Mersham'* (between the Ribble and Mersey). This contrasts with neighbouring Craven which was more thoroughly surveyed and where Kelbrook, Earby, Gisburn and Barnoldswick are all named.

After the Norman Conquest the Hundred of Blackburn was held briefly by Roger de Poitou, and then passed to the **de Lacys**, who built Clitheroe Castle as their local administrative seat and renamed the area the **Honor of Clitheroe**. When the Honor was sub-divided into Manors, Foulridge became part of the Manor of Colne and was referred to variously as the Manor, Lordship or Township of Foulridge. However, unlike Colne which (apart from estates at Alkincoats, Emmott and Barnside) was held personally by the de Lacys, Foulridge was sublet by the military tenure of knight service, originally involving the tenant following his lord into battle for a set number of days in the year, but commuted to a monetary payment at an early date.

Descent of the Manor

The **Lordship of Foulridge** was held successively by *'the three Johns of Foulridge'* in the 1240s by John de Grigleton, in 1275 by John de Poitou, and in 1321 by John de Thornhill. These Norman lords were great barons who also held large estates elsewhere and they would rarely, if ever, have visited Foulridge. The Thornhills held large estates in the Thornhill/Halifax area of West Riding and in Lincolnshire.

The tomb of Sir John de Thornhill, who died in 1321, shows him as a knight in mail armour with his legs crossed indicating that he had fought in the Crusades.

Top: The Thornhill coat of arms.
Below: The Savile coat of arms, featuring three owls.

In 1404 Foulridge descended to the powerful **Savile family** through the marriage of the Thornhill heiress, Elizabeth, to Sir Henry Savile, and the Saviles remained Lords of the Manor for almost two hundred years. The family resided at Thornhill Hall, near Dewsbury. The alabaster tomb of Sir Thomas Savile (c.1447) can be seen in Thornhill Church, as can the oak tomb of 1529 bearing the effigies of Sir John Savile and his two wives. His second wife, Elizabeth Paston, was related to the royal family, and their son, Henry Savile, was an important, almost notorious character in the first half of the 16th century. Like his forbears he was High Sheriff of Yorkshire for several years and was one of the Honourable Council established in the North during the reign of Elizabeth I.

In the second half of the 16th century the Saviles appear to have sold off many parcels of land and subsequent records show fractions of the Manor being held by a number of people. The Manor as a whole disappeared.

What was Foulridge like in the Middle Ages?

When John de Thornhill died in 1322 he held the Lordship of Foulridge directly of the King by homage and the service of the eighth part of a knight's fee. The Manor consisted of:

- one capital messuage (dwelling)
- 8 acres of meadow
- 8 oxgangs of land (i.e. ploughlands) let to tenants-at-will
- 50 acres of rodeland (waste/common)
- 20 shillings rent from 4 free tenants (therefore four cottages), and
- a water corn mill.

An oxgang was a variable measure related to the amount of land an ox could plough in a year and could vary in size enormously (between 7 and 50 acres) depending on the soil quality.

Successive centuries saw the township develop as a number of small hamlets with isolated farmsteads dotted around the surrounding area. The nucleus of village life was **Town Gate** with its village green, well, and stocks, and where each May day the maypole was sited.

How the name 'Foulridge' evolved

1219	Folfric
1246	Folrigge
1275	Florigg, Folerigg
1302	Folering
1311	Folrigg
1542	Fulrigge
1600	Fowlerigge

The name Foulridge is derived from the Old English words '*fola*' meaning foal and '*hrycg*' for ridge, making the most probable meaning '*the ridge where the foals grazed*'.

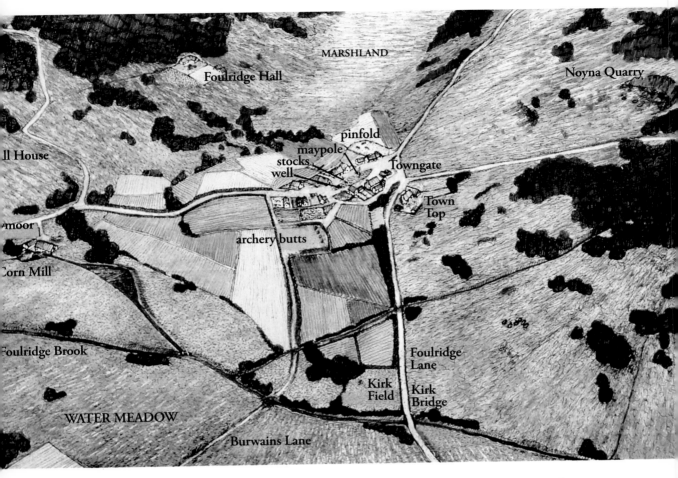

Foulridge Hall
MARSHLAND
Noyna Quarry
ll House
pinfold
maypole
stocks
well
Towngate
Town Top
moor
archery butts
Corn Mill
Foulridge Lane
oulridge Brook
Kirk Field
Kirk Bridge
WATER MEADOW
Burwains Lane

View of Foulridge as it may have appeared in medieval times.

Close by, on land between Croft Mill and Burwains Lane known locally as Bradley Butts, were the **archery targets** where in medieval and early Tudor times every male in the village between the ages of 7 and 60 had to practise archery. The crushing defeat of the French at the Battle of Crecy (1346) by the English archers established the importance of the English longbow and men were obliged by statute to possess a bow and arrows, and every 'tything, village and hamlet' had to have its own archery butts. In 1553 there was a military muster in Lancashire and 8 Foulridge men were required to fight for England. So much importance was attached to archery that other games such as dice, cards, quoits, bowls and tennis and 'all other idle games' (*ludos vanus*) were banned. In 1566 James Mankinhoiles of Folerige and others were fined for assembling and playing with stone bowls.

On the Great House Farm side of Town Gate was the **pinfold** where straying animals were impounded until claimed on payment of a fine. Villagers grazed their sheep and oxen on the common and dug turf for fuel from the waste on the outskirts of the village.

The busiest road out of the village was **Foulridge Lane** which led southwards via Kirk Bridge to Colne where villagers attended church, went to market and used the fulling mill at Colne Waterside. **Red Lane**, the ancient highway from Colne to Clitheroe, bounded the village to the south and was an important manorial road. The site of the Langroyd roundabout was formerly known as King Gate because Red Lane was the beginning of the King's Highway.

Kirk Bridge was so named long before Foulridge Church was built. It takes its name from the fact that the Foulridge or Tailor's Cross (which now stands beside the Cenotaph) was originally sited close by. The cross, which dates to the 13th century, was erected as a preaching cross to provide the people of Foulridge with a field kirk where they could hold open-air services and where funerals could rest on their way to Colne churchyard for burial.

Corn was taken to the lord of the manor's corn mill which was sited near the present Burwain Sailing Club. **The Foulridge water corn mill**, in existence by 1322, was powered by Foulridge Brook which now flows along the base of the reservoir. The mill must have been a very small affair, and we know from Barcroft records that it was thatched. Its millstones came from the top of Noyna and there are still a number of them scattered on the hillside like giant tiddlywinks.

An early mention of the Foulridge Mill occurs in the Duchy of Lancaster Pleadings of June 1591 which record that the corn mill dam head was destroyed during a riot. The bill of complaint states that certain men '*did with bills, halberts, swordes, daggers and other weapons as well offensive as defensyve assemble .... near unto the said water corn milne in Foulridge, and with force and arms in riotous and unlawful manner .... cast in peeces, hale and pull and drawe down the said water corn milne and the dammes and pooles thereto belonging.*'

The mill was obviously rebuilt as it ran for at least a further hundred years. It was then deserted and eventually buried beneath the Reedymoor embankment of the Foulridge Reservoir.

Chapter 3

THE BARCROFT FAMILY

By the second half of the 16th century the Manor of Foulridge had become sub-divided and the principal family to emerge was the Barcrofts. They came to Foulridge from Barcroft Hall at Cliviger, near Burnley at the end of the 16th century and first purchased Foulridge Hall, then Noyna Hall and seemed to alternate between the two. Sometimes the father would be living at Noyna and the eldest son at Foulridge, and sometimes they would reverse the situation. In the middle of the 17th century they also bought Colne Hall, which stood on the site of Carlo's restaurant in Colne.

In 1594 **Ambrose Barcroft** married Mary Hartley of Wellhead at Winewall. Their 3rd son, **William**, born in 1611, married Grace Rycroft of Moss House and they lived at Haigh in the Parish of Thornton. William entered the army under Cromwell, rose to the rank of Major and went to Ireland in 1648. Sometime later his wife and five children were drowned on their way to join him. Barcroft family records claim William was offered an estate in Athlone for his services in the Parliamentarian army but he refused because he had in the meantime become a member of the Society of Friends and could not accept what had been acquired by the sword. The estate was then offered to and accepted by his second-in-command the ancestor of the present Lord Castlemaine. As his second wife

Barcroft Coat of Arms. Argent a lion rampant sable

All that remains of Foulridge Hall is a boundary wall with three carved stone finials above the gateway.

William married Margaret Bernard of Alkincoats and they settled in Ireland. Their children included John Barcroft (b.1664) a well-known Quaker preacher and author who visited Foulridge on several occasions.

William's older brother, and heir to the Barcroft estates in Foulridge, was **Thomas** (b.1607) who married Alice, daughter of John Hargreaves of Heyroyd. Their eldest son, **Ambrose** (1629-1693), attended the old Colne Grammar School and was a contemporary of John Tillotson, later Archbishop of Canterbury. Ambrose was a wool merchant and bought 'packcloths of wool' on a fairly large scale from Lincolnshire and Yorkshire. He rose to eminence when he was appointed *High Constable of the Hundred of Blackburn* in 1681. This was a prestigious position which meant he was the agent of the king in this part of Lancashire, and involved him in many journeys. His register is probably the only surviving detailed account of the work a High Constable and records his responsibilities for a wide area, with constables being answerable to him. Their duties included searching for 'sturdy beggars' to ensure they could be punished and reporting any recusants or Quakers. The Register contains an interesting list of all persons in Foulridge who held property valued at more than four pounds in 1681, and refers to local gentry of the time with whom he had dealings, including the Walmsleys of Dunkenhalgh, Towneleys of Towneley, Shuttleworths of Gawthorpe and Starkie of Huntroyd.

Ambrose also kept a Memoranda book from 1689–1693 (during the reign of William and Mary) in which he recorded notable events in the district such as the fact that Dutch Dragoons were quartered with him in 1689 and the visit of his cousin, John Barcroft (the celebrated Quaker preacher of Kings County, Ireland) in October 1690.

The Diary and Accounts of Ambrose Barcroft's only son **Thomas** (1653-1732) also survive and, together with the aforementioned documents, are preserved at the Lancashire Record Office.

The Barcroft family was involved in the running of the **Foulridge Water Corn Mill**, and Thomas recorded how the millstones were brought down from Noyna in the 1690s. A hole was chiselled through the centre of each millstone and a pair stood on edge whilst a tree trunk was driven through to form a contraption resembling a grotesque bobbin to be taken down the hill - a process which involved ingenuity and the help of three men, two horses and eight oxen. A careless nudge may have sent the stones careering at full speed into the unsuspecting village below.

Part-worked millstones near the quarry at Noyna.

Thomas tried to keep the mill going in its last working, but unprofitable, years. In around 1694 he was threatened with a Chancery Court action by the holder of one fifth of the Foulridge mill and, in response, he wrote that: "*I have never heard of anybody ever concn'd in it but they were losers by it, and I can have the testimony of ye whole Cuntry that it never was good for anything .... and now since Pollard built the Mill at Woodend nobody own'd it (for it was short of water and without a drying killn) .... I had put it into good repair at £20 charges at least .... so that I may safely affirm that I am £40 loser by it. You may cause me to spend money and spend your owne, but to avoid a Chancery Sute I am content to give you a Guiny, tho it may be in my owne wrong, there is likewise a Millrope, a good one, and a wire siff you may have. I wonder you should expect I keep up the mill after I had sold the two millstones to Mr Hoyle*".

In the early 1700s the same Thomas Barcroft hid some money on Noyna, near where the millstones are. This was in the days before banks and when finding a safe place to hoard money was quite a problem. The money was found and classed as **treasure trove** and Thomas had quite a lengthy job recovering his money.

During the latter half of the 1700s **John Barcroft of Noyna** (1727-1782) was the Steward of Clitheroe Castle and presided over the local courts at Higham and Colne. He married Elizabeth, daughter and co-heiress of his cousin William Barcroft of Noyna and Foulridge Hall. His son and heir, **Ambrose William Barcroft** (1759-1795) joined the army and served in America during the War of Independence, and also on the continent. A few months after his return from the Siege of Nijmegen in Holland he was ordered to the West Indies in the war against France and, when his regiment came to recruit locally, so popular was the young Captain that the men of the district queued two deep through the streets of Colne to enlist.

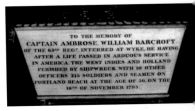

Memorial in Colne Parish Church to Captain Ambrose William Barcroft.

Tragically the convoy of ships, which left the Isle of Wight on 15 November 1795, had only reached the Dorset coast when it was overtaken by one of the most violent storms ever recorded. The ship that carried Captain Barcroft and his men was **the Piedmont**, and of the 150 on board, only 12 survived. Letters written by the ship's surgeon, Lt Shrapnel, to relatives contain this account of the morning after the disaster: "*I rode down to the beach and crossed the Fleet water in the hope of identifying some of the unfortunate victims of the storm. The horror of the scene infinitely passed expectation, for more than two miles of beach was literally strewn with dead bodies, and to my sorrow and amazement I saw a group of local people collecting plundered goods that had been stole from the mangled corpses of the dead*". Captain Barcroft's body was recognized by the scars he had received in the service of his country.

It was some time before news of the catastrophe reached Colne and, when the total loss of life was realized, there was general mourning, particularly in Colne Waterside where hardly a household was unaffected.

Captain Barcroft's daughter, **Ellen**, was only 12 months old when he died and she was the last of the Foulridge line of the Barcrofts. When she married Edward Parker of Alkincoats in 1816, the Parker family inherited the former Barcroft lands in Foulridge and became the principal landowner in the village.

Portrait of Ellen Barcroft at Browsholme Hall.

The Lordship of Foulridge appears to have been linked to Foulridge Hall and when Robert 'Bobby' Pickles acquired Foulridge Hall Farm in 1920 he also acquired the title of Lord of the Manor. On selling the property in the early 1950s the Pickles family retained the title and the manorial rights.

Chapter 4

FARMING

Looking across Foulridge Reservoir towards Blacko and Pendle it is difficult to imagine that this valley has ever looked otherwise. The canal works have been for so long a part of the local scene that we can scarcely imagine the appearance of the valley before they came – when instead of the great expanse of water there was a diminutive dam and a tiny corn mill just above the point on the present embankment nearest to Cocker Hill. Sloping gently down to this ancient mill were the *Foulridge Ings* – a quiet succession of water meadows belonging to the various farmsteads of Foulridge which were approached by the steep lane which still leads off to the village from the walk round the reservoir bank. The lowest of the meadows – the nearest to the mill – was reserved for '*the Poor of Foulridge*'.

Old field names such as *Bean Royd* and *Potato Piece* indicate that the village was far more self sufficient than today. The heavy soil was improved by spreading marl (chalky earth), sand and later lime. The nearest market was Colne, where they sold what they produced and bought whatever they required.

Haymaking at Cragg Nook, 1945/6. Photo by Thomas Robinson.
Foreground L-R Alan Veevers, James 'Jimmy' Ralph in the centre, Roy Wildman (his grandson) on right. On top of the hayrick Sydney Cox. Jimmy Ralph had farmed Waller Hill from the early 1920s.

Before the coming of cotton in the 19th century, farming was the main occupation. **Whitemoor** was typical of Pennine farming - an area of moorland with scattered farms and cottages. The farms varied in size – some no more than 10 acres and the largest 50 to 60. It was a hard existence - no electricity or milking machines, just storm lanterns for light in the barns, and paraffin lamps for the house. Small farms didn't even have mowing machines; the grass was cut by long poled scythes, worked into hay by the farmer and his family, and carted loose into the barn. Cream was churned to produce butter usually by the farmer's wife or daughters. Cattle were mainly the big Shorthorns with maybe a few Ayrshires. Now the majority of dairy cows are Friesians.

In 1902 68 farms were listed under Foulridge. Some were within the old 'Foulridge Detached' which passed to Colne in 1935. By 1937 there were still 59 farms of which 20 were described as *'Poultry'*. Today there are only a handful of working farms - mainly pastoral in beef and sheep.

Jean and Chester Kneller, outside the barn at Accornlee, 1958 the year after they married.

Poultry Farming

By the 1930s poultry farming was particularly important locally. David Alderson kept hens on land behind the Hare & Hounds (where the old folks bungalows are now), John Whalley at Accornlee House and there were numerous smallholdings.

There were also **hatcheries** which specialised in incubating chickens which were then 'sexed' (i.e. their sex determined) to separate hens from cocks. The hen chicks were then crated and exported in vast numbers to all parts of the UK through Foulridge station, and the cock chicks were sold cheaply to be reared as 'table birds'.

Sydney Benson's hatchery at Reedymoor Terrace was affectionately referred to as "The Incubator Place". It was sufficiently important to warrant bringing electricity to Reedymoor Terrace at a time when oil lamps were still the main form of lighting. Before the war Vincent Benson came from Cowling every Tuesday to sex the chickens, succeeded by Ronnie Hook after the war. The old barn at Reedymoor Terrace has recently (2009) undergone conversion by Malcolm Benson and is named *'The Old Hatchery'* in memory of its former use.

Edwin Storey, also of Reedymoor Terrace, kept hens behind Ball House. The Colne Times of 11 November 1936 reported that *'Colne Brigade was called to a blazing hen cabin at the Mooreside Poultry Farm, Reedymoor last Saturday night. The cabin was totally destroyed. The fire is believed to be due to the exploding of a paraffin brooder. The cabin contained four brooders, in each of which there were 200 eggs, the damage amounting to about £100.'*

Sidney Spencer of Cragg House, and George Brooks of Skipton Old Road were partners in the thriving firm of '**Brooks & Spencer**'. Edwin Waterworth of Belmont Terrace was taken into their employment as a sort of apprentice, and the firm went to considerable expense to have him trained by a Japanese expert in the art of sexing chickens. He became so adept at that he could certify 90% plus the difference between hen and cock 'day old' chicks. The Japanese went home when war was declared but 'chicken sexing' was so important that it was a reserved occupation and exempt from all forms of military service.

After the war **Jack Whitaker** kept poultry and rented two acres of his great

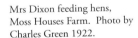

Mrs Dixon feeding hens, Moss Houses Farm. Photo by Charles Green 1922.

Great House Farm.

grandad's land at Breeze House; "*the same two acres where I had begun in 1930*".

Poultry farming gradually declined locally. By 1949 Allen Lane at Noyna, and Edwin Waterworth were two of only 11 poultry men in the village. **Ronnie Hook** and his wife Mary subsequently continued the chicken sexing tradition, and were in great demand travelling hundreds of miles each week into both Cheshire and North Yorkshire.

Great House Farm

Deeds to Great House date to 1551 when it was owned by Robert Hammond. The building bears a date stone of 1660. Over the centuries the property descended to Robinsons, Pollards, and Heatons. The farm had its own smithy and fields with names such as Kiln Croft, Midecocks Ing, Spreadwife Banks and Ark Riding.

In 1847 some land was sold off to the Leeds & Bradford Railway Extension (Shipley to Colne), and the remaining 41 acres to Hartley Parkinson of Colne, Spirit Merchant. The Threlfalls of Moorlands bought Great House in 1890 and let it to James Littlefair. William Roberts bought the property in the early 1920s and farmed it himself assisted by Abner Brunskill Barritt then living at nearby Ormerod Terrace. James Slinger was the farmer in 1949.

In recent years the property has been substantially renovated and split to form several domestic dwellings.

Lark Hill

The barn at Lark Hill contains an owl hole, more picturesquely known locally as a 'hullit hoil' which provided access for owls to protect the grain from rodents.

Lark Hill was owned by the Smiths of Springfield in the 19th C and later by the Pickles family. In the late 1800s the farm was tenanted by **Jim Foulds** described as "*the local cow doctor, called in whenever an animal needed treatment, his main remedy for healing wounds and sores etc. was to rub raw salt in. The farmers wives used to say when he appeared 'That cruel man is here again', but he must have known that there was no better antiseptic at that time. In those days there was a well on the roadside opposite County Brook Lane, and having no water in the buildings, he made his poor old wife, with two buckets carry water for his stock and the house from this well, no little distance. He used to stand at the farm gate shouting 'Off tha goes lass*"

The owl hole at Lark Hill barn.

Long Hill

Long Hill Farm has connections with Ball House dating back more than 350 years. The Walton family occupied both properties throughout the 1700s, and today they are both owned by John Bank. The Smith family of Netherheys in Colne acquired Long Hill in 1870.

Edmund 'Ned' Crabtree was the farmer in the 1890s and, other than a brief interlude in the 1920s when Craven Wilson tenanted Long Hill, the farm was run by the Crabtree family for several generations.

More recently **Jack Judson** farmed Long Hill (for almost sixty years from 1940-1998). He recollected that there was no farmhouse at Long Hill and he converted the old dairy into a house. It seems that the earlier farmhouse at Long Hill had

been demolished, possibly to provide privacy for the owners of Springfield, and the farmer lived at nearby Mount View.

Tom Smith lived at Springfield until 1925 when the property was acquired by the Pickles. It seems the Smiths retained Long Hill Farm until 1949 when it was bought by the Nelson family.

Cocker Hill

The Wilson family have farmed Cocker Hill for three generations and provided the village with a friendly milkman for more than 80 years. Craven Wilson bought the farm in 1932, succeeded by Alan in the 1950s, followed by Andrew. Alan also dealt in tractors and this activity is perpetuated by Stan Storey who operates a tractor firm from the farm

Alan bought Ball House Farm in 1963. He retained the land and farm buildings but subsequently sold Ball House to Roland Halstead.

Craven is a Wilson family name. Andrew has it as his christian name, and has continued the tradition by naming his son Richard Craven George.

Above left: Long Hill Farm c.1900. Photo by Ernest Spivey.

Above: Craven and Mary Wilson with children Alan, Ethel and Hilda c.1927 Craven Wilson came from Black Lane Ends to Long Hill in the early 1920s. Alan was born at Long Hill in 1925.

Below left: Ridgehill, Cocker Hill under construction. Harold, Alan and Craven Wilson, late 1952. The Wilsons built Ridgehill as a family home for Alan and his wife, Margaret, who married in April 1953.

Below: Alan, Andrew, Elizabeth and Valerie Wilson outside Ball House barn (now Mistals) c.1964.

The Edmondson twins, Johnnie and Jim c.1950s. Johnnie drove for Walton Barritt.

Noyna Bottom Farm

Nestling in the hillside of Noyna, the farm was affectionately known in the early 1900s as 'the Sweetshop on Noyna' where walkers could buy either cups or jugs of tea. The farm was used in 1968 for a scene in 'the Tenant of Wildfell Hall' in which it became the Rose & Crown Inn.

Reedymoor Farm

The name Reedymoor is from the Old English *hreod* for reed, rush or reed-bed plus the OE *mor* for barren land, moor or marshland making '*a marsh overgrown with reeds*'. Reedymoor Farm was built around 1580 with additions made in the late 1600s. The Colne Parish Registers record a christening from Reedymoor in 1603, then spelled '*Ridimore*', when the house was occupied by **the Walton family**. Throughout the late 1600s and late 1700s the house was owned by the **Hartleys**, succeeded by Joseph Priestly in 1807. The property remained in the **Priestly-Midgley** family until the mid 1900s but was latterly let to tenant farmers.

Reedymoor Farm.

By 1879 **David Wilkinson** from Cowling, then aged 26, was tenanting the farm. When he retired, he removed to his newly built **Reedymoor Terrace**, and his nephew 'Jim' Wilkinson took over the tenancy and remained at Reedymoor for more than 30 years.

Reedymoor remained a working farm until 1965 when it became the residence of **Stephen Pickles**. Apparently part of the house had remained closed up for years and was only brought back into use just before **Des and Pauline Connolly** acquired the property in 1977. They converted it into B&B accommodation and recounted numerous tales of spooky happenings in the house.

Reedymoor Terrace

In about 1903, **David Wilkinson** bought a field from the Ball House estate for £400, and by 1913 had built the five houses on Reedymoor Terrace to provide a home for each of his surviving children. His son, David Wilkinson Jnr moved into the Terrace on his marriage to Maggie Jolly in 1918. To this day Wilkinson descendants still occupy houses in the Terrace, and this quiet backwater (facing open fields which can never be built on as they are over the canal tunnel) has changed little in the last hundred years.

Reedymoor Terrace.

Towngate Farm

The farmhouse occupied 15-19 Towngate by the side of Joe Lane. The farm was also known as Foulridge Farm, and in more recent times as Dixon's after the family who tenanted the farm in the early 1900s.

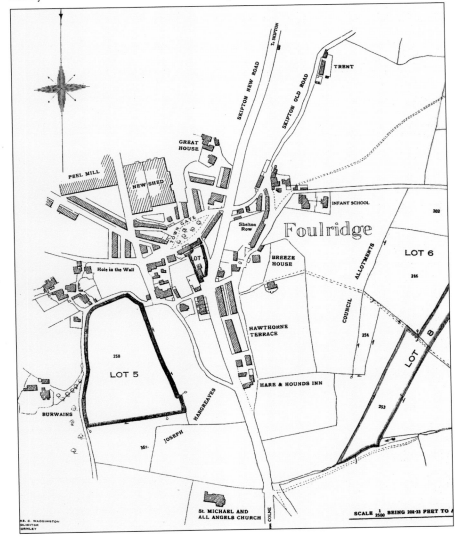

Detail from Sale Plan for Town Gate or Simpson's Farm. 1928 Lot 4 was described as:'The freehold Farm House, No. 17 Towngate, the Store adjoining, being No. 19, and the cottage, No.15 Towngate; together with excellent farm buildings which include a shippon for 10 head, Barn, Stable for two horses, manure shed, piggery & yard ... Occupied by George Dixon'.

Hey

In the 1700s the name Hey appeared variously as *Hey*, *Ye Hey*, *Th'Hay* and *Foulridge Hey*.

Hey Farm has been in the same family – **the Barritts** – for at least 260 years. A John Barritt is recorded as living at Hey in 1742 and the property descended through his son Robert to the present Barritts of Hey.

The farmer in the late 1800s was Hartley Barritt who also kept the New Inn at Foulridge and had boats on the canal transporting coal, stone etc. Four of his sons helped with the business while the eldest, John Henry, farmed with his grandmother Ann at Hey. He married Dora Ann Yates who came from another long established Whitemoor family. The family had strong connections with Mount Pleasant Chapel which had been founded by Hartley Barritt's great uncle John Barritt.

Aug 2009 photo of Barritt trailer with Hey Farm in background.

Chapter 5

FOULRIDGE PLACE NAMES

A surprising amount of information about the history of the village can be gleaned from its place names.

KEY
OE - Old English (Anglo-Saxon)
ON - Old Norse
OWSc - Old West Scandinavian

Olr - Old Irish
ME - Middle English

ABNER ROW / TERRACE
Probably named after the builder. Abner was a popular name locally.

AB'S GINNEL
The lane beside Breeze House leading to the allotments, named after Abner Barrett who farmed the land in the early 1900s.

ACCORNLEE / ACCORNLEY
1259 Akerlandeleye, 1608 Accrondley, 1621 Acranley / Acornley, 1660 Accronley Eilert Ekwall, the leading authority on Lancashire place names gives the meaning as being ME for 'acre land, ploughed or arable land'. The name literally means '*clearing in an oak forest*' suggesting an early clearing of woodland for cultivation purposes.

ALMA AVENUE
Unlike the Alma Inn at Laneshawbridge which was named in commemoration of the famous battle, Alma Avenue has nothing to do with the Crimean War. It was named after the first residents of the road - **Al**bert and **Ma**ry Barnes.

Right: Albert and Mary Barnes, after whom Alma Avenue gained its name.

ARCHERY AVENUE
The field on which the houses were built in the 1990s was earlier known as Bradley Butts, literally '*the broad clearing used for archery practice*' – the site of archery targets in medieval and Tudor times.

ARTISTS' COTTAGE
Nickname given to Scroggin Hall in Victorian times when it became a popular subject for local artists.

BACK HILL
An earlier name for Long Hill referred to in the 1842 Tithe Award.

BACK LANE
Lane which led from Laithe Ends to Waller Hill

BACK O' TH' EDGE
Between Red Lane and Burwains Reservoir, the back of Colne Edge.

BALDWIN'S CORNER / LANE
Opposite the Hole in the Wall, between Laithe Ends Corner and Cocker Hill, named after James Baldwin founder of Baldwin's Charity.

BALL BRIDGE FARM
Earlier name for Blue Slate Farm. The original site was at the bottom of Smithy Lane, nearer to the Canal House beside the ford, but when Burwains Reservoir was built it was removed to the present site.

BALL HOUSE
1581 Bawlhous, 1648 Baulehouse
May derive from the ME word '*balgh*' for rounded, indicating that it was built on a rounded hillock. Alternatively Celtic for an abode. The word ball also has the meaning 'boundary'. This is the more likely meaning of Ball Bridge, beside the ford at the bottom of Smithy Lane. The stream formed the boundary between Colne and Foulridge.

BANK HOUSE
At the bottom of Stoney Lane - formerly Martin's Bank.

BARNSIDE
1258 Bernesete. ON *saetr* (shieling, sheep pasture) '*Biorn's mountain pasture*'.
A considerable estate in the former Foulridge Detached portion which stretched from Laneshawbridge, beyond Black Lane Ends to the Yorkshire border.

BAR BECK
The stream which flowed beside the Foulridge Toll Bar

BELL TERRACE
Old name for Belmont Terrace, named after Alexander Bell, the owner of the land on which the terrace was built.

Detail of datestone on Belmont Terrace

BERRY'S MILL
Croft Mill, after former owner, William Berry.

BLACK BROOK
Earlier name for County Brook 'black' having the meaning of boundary. The stream formed the old county border between Yorkshire and Lancashire prior to 1974.

BLUE SLATE FARM
Formerly known as Ball Bridge Farm, but renamed after the new blue slates which were being introduced at the time.

BOGGART BRIDGE
One time nickname for Kirk Bridge, traditionally haunted by the tailor killed nearby.

BORDIN LANE
Corruption of Baldwin Lane

BOTTOMS
Local name for the triangular depression between Foulridge and Salterforth, remnants of former fenlands now drained.

BREEZE HOUSE

A popular theory is that when first built the farm stood in a very exposed position and the wind caught it from every direction. A similar idea is expressed in other local names such as Windy Harbour in Trawden and Coldweather in Nelson.

BROACH

There are three farms of this name - Higher Broach, Lower Broach and Broach Flatt (known locally as Flatts). The name could possibly originate from the OE brec 'land broken up for cultivation' or the Scandinavian brekka for 'slope, hill'.

BULL FIELD

A former Breeze House field name. The field was enclosed by stone walling as opposed to hedgerow and fence. Until the late 18th century bull-baiting took place close by.

BURWAIN(S)

OE byrgan/burgaesn 'burial, cairn, burial ground' suggesting some ancient burial, possibly a barrow yet to be discovered. Alternatively from the OE burwe for 'circle', a stone circle also implying a burial. It is also possible the mound could have been a boundary marker. The name is interesting as it is usually given to sites which bore evidence of ancient occupation. Spelled 'Burrons' on the 1842 Tithe Award Map.

CARR'S ROAD / TEDDY CARR DRIVE

The private road from Accornlee to Kelbrook Moor constructed by Edward Carr of Langroyd at the turn of the last century to enable him to reach his Shooting Box on the moor.

CAT FOLD

Originally part of Foulridge Farm on Towngate. Possibly a reference to wild cats or ferrets which still roamed the district in the 1770s, but more likely to have its origin in OE cata meaning sheep pen, or perhaps simply an abbreviation for cattle fold.

CAUSEWAY

A paved way long before paving became the norm, indicating a road formerly of some importance.

The name may originate from being a causeway connecting low lying areas with firm ground.

CHAPEL STREET / STEPS

Reminders of the Wesleyan Methodist Chapel which occupied the site for 160 years until the early 1980s.

CLONDIKE / KLONDIKE

Nickname for the WWI munitions dump sited between the Canal and Barnoldswick New Road. No apparent connection with the region in northwest Canada famed for the Gold Rush which started in 1897.

COCKER HILL

The most likely meaning is *the crooked or winding hill* from the OE kukra which is a very apt description. Other suggested meanings are:
- 'the cock ridge', i.e. the chief ridge or big hill
- OE *cocc* 'cock' probably referring to the woodcock, a bird which was netted for food in the middle ages, suggesting the meaning 'the hill frequented by woodcock'

CORNSHAW BROOK

The name has appeared variously as Cornshaw and Cronshaw for centuries. Even today the spelling alternates on OS maps, Electoral Rolls, Census etc.

CRAGG

A steep or precipitous rugged rock, of Celtic origin.

CRAGG END

Earlier name for Cragg Nook

CRAGG NOOK

The term 'nook' generally applies to a triangular or secluded piece of land.

CROMWELL'S CROFT

Earlier name for Cromwell Street, so named because Cromwell's troops are said to have been billeted in the croft. The old row of cottages originally possessed its own croft immediately opposite.

CRONSHAW BROOK
OE *cranuc* (crane). '*Stream beside the cranes' wood*'. See also Cornshaw Brook.

CRUMMEL SQUARE
Alternative form of Cromwell Row appearing in the 1851 Census.

DANDY END OF BELMONT
Local name for Ivegate, the lane between Belmont Terrace and the New Inn. Prior to Belmont Terrace being built, the Foulridge Dandy Shop occupied the site.

DAUBERS
It has been suggested that the name could derive from OE *beorg*/ON *berg* (hill) and Fr *d'aube* for dawn meaning 'the hill where day broke', but the latter is unlikely as the influence on local names of Norman French was very small. The name may originate from being the home of a man who specialized in 'daub & wattle' construction. The fact that Dauber's Dole, one of Foulridge's oldest charities, founded by John Milner who was described as a 'plasterer' seems to support this theory.

Daubers.

DUKERIES
Nickname for Flatt Gardens, near Broach Flat Farm, on the way to Noyna. They were abandoned c.1920 after being fruit gardens for about 30 years. The owners until the 1880s were the Carrs of Langroyd.

EARL HALL
The hall/cottage occupied by a Norse nobleman. We know that Norsemen settled in the Barnside area but, as *Eorl* was also an OE personal name, and 'Earl' came to be used as a title after the Norman Conquest, it is difficult to know which of these meanings should be assumed.

EDMUND'S VILLA
Possibly the site of some former holy place connected with the martyr king, the name appearing as St Edmunds villa on an early map; but Edmund was a common Anglo-Saxon name and it is more likely that the place may have been originally settled by a man of that name.

The name Edmunds Villa formerly applied to a cluster of old buildings which later became known as Waller Hill. The 1901 Census lists ten separate properties housing 44 people. A single property now perpetuates the name.

Detail from the Foulridge Tithe Award Map 1842.

FLAG ALLEY
Nickname for Stoney Court.

Stoney Lane

FLAT TOPS
The houses on Skipton Road beside Burwains Reservoir built in the 1930s may have pitched roofs these days, but they will always be known as the 'Flat Tops'.

FOOT PAD TOP
Earlier name for Causeway Top on Noyna.

FOULRIDGE
1219 Folfric, 1246 Folrigge, 1261 Folrig, 1542 Fulrigge, 1600 Fowlerigge

Not derived from evil smelling, but from the OE *fola* meaning foal plus *hrycg* for ridge making the meaning '*the ridge where the foals grazed*' or possibly 'the foal's back' owing to some likeness between the shape of the hill to one.

FOULRIDGE DETACHED
The name given to the Monkroyd, Barnside and Laneshawbridge area which, until 1935 boundary reorganisation, was part of Foulridge although being physically 'detached' from it.

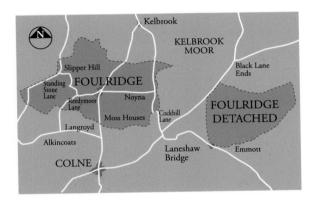

FOULRIDGE HEY
Old alternative form of Hey

GILES CORNER / GILES YARD
One-time nickname for Foulridge Farm after Giles Hitchin, the farmer before the Second World War.

GREENHEAD
Earlier name for Moorlands

GREENWOOD'S CORNER
On Skipton New Road at the junction with Causeway, the site of Greenwood's bakery and confectionery shop, tea and refreshment rooms in the early 1900s.

GRINNING RAT
The public house at Wanless which catered for the navvies who came to repair the Foulridge Tunnel in 1824. Some say the name originated from a plague of rats which bedevilled the project, but 'Grinning Rat' is a common pub name chosen by navvies and others with nautical connections.

HAGUE
OE *haga*. Originally a hedge, especially hawthorn, later 'a place surrounded by a hedge'. Some enclosures were used to prevent animals straying and it has been suggested that the original Hague may have been an ancient enclosure for oxen connected with nearby Oxenards.

HALLAM MOOR
Named after the Hallam family who lived at nearby Moorlands at the end of the 19th century.

HATCHET LANE
Extension of Watery Lane towards Castle Road. A corruption of 'Hat shop'. In the 1840s a hatter lived there.

HATTERS BRIDGE
Another reminder of Foulridge's once flourishing felt hat-making industry.

HEARL / HEART HALL
Hearl Hall is marked on a pre 1905 map of Foulridge, and **Heart** Hall appears in Barrett's Directories, as being farmed in 1899 & 1902 by Wm Davis. Both seem to be misspellings as William Davies appears in the 1901 Census at **Earl** Hall between Knarrs and Barnside.

HEY, HEY FOLD & GREAT HEY
Similar in meaning to Hague, being originally '*a place surrounded by a hedge*' or '*enclosure*', which in Anglo-Saxon times could have been clearings in the forest where the people lived and cattle grazed.

HEY MILL
Earlier name for County Brook Mill.

HIGHFIELD AVENUE
Built on land previously part of Breeze House Farm known as High Meadow

HOBSTONES
'*Hob*' is OE for hobgoblin or devil suggesting the meaning of 'Devil's stones' and there is certainly a history of haunting.
In the 1500s the farm's name was spelt *Hobbey*stones and this suggests alternative origins - 'Hobby' the name for a small falcon and also for a small horse. Bearing in mind that Foulridge gained its name from being the ridge where foals grazed, could the name be horse stones rather than devil stones? It is certainly plausible but doesn't explain the puzzle of the stones or the mysterious happenings at Hobstones.

HOLLINGHURST
OE *hurst* (thick wood, forest, wooded hill) '*The grove of holly trees*'.

HULLET HALL, HULLET NEST
Hullet is vernacular for Owl.

INTAKE (FARM)
1575 Intack, 1600 Intacke
Intake is a general term for land newly taken into cultivation, either from a moor or common, frequently used at the time of enclosure. The name suggests that Intake Farm was originally part of Noyna Common. Foulridge National School was built on land known as Further Intake.

IVEGATE
'*Road to the water*' - it led to Low Well on Town Gate, the main source of drinking water in the village

JOANNA'S CHAPEL
Now demolished barn sited behind Blenheim Terrace once used by locally thriving sect of British Israelites, named after Joanna Southcott.

JOE LANE
Abbreviation for Joseph's Lane leading to Town Gate

JOSEPH'S PLACE
Four acres of 'waste' land adjoining Kelbrook Moor, near the Shooting Box, formerly '*the Town's piece of land on the moors*'. Possibly in earlier days a small piece of common land without an owner. The land was leased by the Parish Council to Edward Carr and eventually sold to his executors in 1924.

KINGS HOUSES
Listed in the 1901 Census between Standing Stone Gate and Hill Top. Also appears on OS maps of the period as Smith's Cottages.

KIRK BRIDGE
So named long before Foulridge Church was built. It takes its name from the fact that the Foulridge or Tailor's Cross was originally sited close by.

KIRK FIELD
The field where the Foulridge Cross was sited, and where anciently open air services were held - a field kirk.

KIRK RISE
Original name for the Manor House.

KIT SYKE
The name of the old well on Town Top from OE *sic* / ON *sik* (ditch, small stream, watercourse).

LAITHE ENDS CORNER
ON *hlatha* (barn). Laithe Ends is located beside Croft Mill between two old barns.

LAKE BURWAIN

A rather pretentious misnomer. The 'lake' is in fact one of the compensation reservoirs for the Leeds & Canal. Its correct name is Foulridge Lower Reservoir.

LANCASHIRE GHYLL
ON *gill* (narrow valley). The valley divided Yorkshire and Lancashire prior to boundary reorganization in 1974.

LAVEROCK HILL
Earlier name for Lark Hill. Laverock is vernacular for skylark. '*The hill frequented by larks*'.

LITTLE CHURCH BRIDGE BROOK
Former name for Bar Beck. Another reminder of the open church held in nearby kirk field.

LOW ROW / LOW LANE
Cromwell Street. Abner Terrace was known as Top Row.

LOWTHER LANE
Pronounced *Lother* Lane by older generations. OIr *lothr* means 'a canal' and it may have gained its name from Irish navvies who worked on the canal, or originate from the ON *laur* for 'froth, foaming river'. It is equally plausible that it was simply the lane leading to the lower village (as opposed to Town Top) and Low Well.

MANOR HOUSE
Traditionally the name Manor House was linked with lord of the manor, who had various rights over the land and his tenants, but this modern house has no such associations.

MERECLOUGH
OE *maere* (boundary) and OE *cloh* (a steep sided valley). '*Boundary valley*'.

MIDGE HOLE/HOIL
There are various explanations for the origin of its name:
- from its diminutive size
- a place infested with midges (insects)
- dialect mudge hole (boggy), or
- a corruption of 'Midgley's Mill' from a connection with the Midgley family who owned a great deal of land in the Wood End/County Brook area.

'MILE' TUNNEL
This nickname for the Foulridge Tunnel is really a double misnomer. It is 120 yards short of being a mile long, and much of it wasn't tunnelled at all, but was constructed on the 'cut and cover' method after the navvies encountered quick sands.

MILL LANE
Between Station Road and Warehouse Lane. It led to Lonsdale's Peel Mill.

MISTALS
OE for shippon. The house was converted from the old barn at Ball House.

MONKEY RACK
Beside Greenwood's Corner at the top of Causeway – the landing stage on which was unloaded the flour ground at County Brook corn mill.

MONKROYD

'*The monks' clearing*'. The Barnside estate was granted to the Monks of Pontefract in 1258.

MONTE CARLO

Old nickname for Noyna Quarries after the gambling activities which took place there.

MOSS FARM

also known as Moss House and Foulridge Moss (now Hollybush). OE *mos* / ON *mosi* for a marshy place indicates the original landscape.

NOYNA

1589 Noynow Cragg, 1602 Noynowe, 1614 Noonow, 1627 Nonowe, 1645 Noynay, 1786 Noona   deriving from OE *noon* + *hoh*, meaning literally '*the noon hill*' probably so named by the earliest settlers in the district (at Thornton in Craven), Noyna being directly south of their settlement and the sun at noon appearing to them to be at its highest point above the hill.

NOYNA WOOD

Noyna Rocks are now shorn of trees, but a document of 1860 suggests that the hill was very much more covered with trees than it is now. It was then referred to as 'The Noyna Wood' or 'Plantation'.

ORMEROD TERRACE

Named after John Ormerod, Quarry Master, Builder and Contractor who built the terrace at the end of the 19th century, and lived at No. 2

OXENARDS

Both a local surname and place name deriving from oxen-herd. The name suggests that oxen, once the main beast of burden and essential for ploughing and carting, pastured here. Oxen were used to bring down the heavy millstones from the top of Noyna.

PEEL MILL

Presumably after Sir Robert Peel, who died in 1850.

PILGRIM'S

Recently revived former nickname for Noyna Mede, the home of Mr W A Pilgrim in the early 20th century.

PROCTER'S CORNER

A reminder of when the village had a shop on almost every corner, the owner's name being used to identify the location.

Margaret and Tom Procter outside their grocer's shop on Station Road.

PURSE

A field adjoining Reef Edge originally infested with Shepherd's purse weed.

RAKE

The road leading to Noyna between Scroggin Hall and the old school, 'Up Rake' as it was locally known, was a very rough road in early days. The term rake is from the OE *hraca* (sheep or cattle walk) and generally applies to a steep road up the hillside.

RED LANE

From the reddish colour of the sandstone which forms Colne Edge.

REEDYMOOR

1603 Reedymore, 1673 Reedimore, 1681 Ridimore. Reedymoor derives from the OE *hreod* for reed, rush or reed-bed plus the OE *mor* for barren land, moor or marshland making '*a marsh overgrown with reeds*'.

REEF EDGE

A field name on early maps of Foulridge.   A reeve was the local supervisor responsible for the running of the Manor. Reef Edge was part of the Foulridge Hall estate.

SALTERSYKE

One of a number of 'salt' names along the Lidgett/ Black Lane Ends road which remind us of the saltways which from monastic to recent times spread from the salt '*wiches*' of Cheshire, NE and East across the Pennines.

SAND HALL

1708 Sand Hoall, 1781 Sand Holme, 1843 Sand Hole

A name deriving from the sand deposits left by the glaciers. The site of a pit from which farmers obtained sand to marl their fields as a means of improving heavy soil.

SCROGGIN HALL

Hall in 16th century dialect refers not to a lofty mansion but to a shepherd's cottage. Another word from the same dialect is *scrogg* which is Nordic in origin and refers to a cleft in rock. Scroggin Hall was therefore very aptly named being literally '*a shepherd's cottage cleft in rock*'.

SHIRT NECK HARRY

Smithy Lane, which leads from the ford at Ball Bridge to Red Lane, is better known locally as Shirt Neck Harry after the man who lived at Blue Slate Farm in Victorian times. He was never seen wearing a collar and tie, not even on the Sabbath, and he was apparently in the habit of chasing people with his stick down the lane which, over the years, became known by his own nickname.

SKELTON ROW, 22-34 Skipton Old Road

Old maps and property deeds show the name to have originally been 'Shelton' Row. The name suddenly changed in the early 1930s when the sign was moved from the middle to the end cottage.

SKIPTON OLD ROAD

The original road to Skipton which became the 'old' road when the new Colne & Broughton turnpike road was constructed in 1824.

SLIP INN

Old inn at the Foulridge end of the Mile Tunnel which catered for bargees and the men who worked on Foulridge wharf. Perhaps aptly named – if they drank too much they risked slipping into the canal.

The former Slip Inn.

SLIPPER HILL

Referred to as *Slipprie Hill* on a map of 1581 - this probably explains the origin.

SMITH'S COTTAGES

Name appearing on the 1912 OS Map, after the Smith family who owned nearby Springfield and Long Hill. Now called Springfield Cottages.

SMITHY LANE

Correct name for Shirt Neck Harry, probably so named because there was a smithy in the vicinity of Blue Slate Farm, known for many years as Smithy House. It has also been suggested that the lane may have some connection with the Smythe family of Edge (now Red Lane) and Sandhole in the 1600s.

SOAP ROW

Local nickname for Pleasant View because the soap on washing day ran down from the cottages into the village.

SOOT ING

A former Great House Farm field name, close to another named Coal Field, suggesting that coal was once extracted here.

SPRING ROW / VIEW
Numbers 1, 3, 5 & 7 Warehouse Lane.

SPRINGFIELD
There is a spring beneath the house

STEW MILL
Old nickname for County Brook Mill from the stewing down of oak bark to make charcoal and dyes.

SUMMIT TUNNEL
The correct name for the Foulridge Tunnel, standing 487 feet above sea level and at the highest section of the waterway.

TAILOR'S CROSS
Probably a corruption of *Tal-lers* Cross, after the Knights Hospitallers who held land at nearby Alkincoats.

TENTER FIELD
Former field name at Hobstones indicating a field where cloth was straightened and dried under tension on tenter frames.

THATCH
The 1851 Census records a property of this name in the Town Gate area, the name probably signifying that the building was, or had originally been, thatched.

THROSTLE NEST
Throstle is vernacular for song thrush.

TIN TAB
The nickname given to the Weavers' Institute which bought the corrugated building once used by Earby church - the 'Tin Tabernacle', latterly the premises of Causeway Joinery.

TOM CROSS
a commonly used boundary stone appellation.

TOP O'TH HILL
Appears in 1901 Census - Hill Top.

TOP ROW
Abner Terrace

TOWNGATE / TOWN GATE
Gate was not a barrier but is from the ON word for *road* or *way*. Town Gate was '*the main street*' of the village.

TOWN TOP
A name dating to medieval times when this was literally the topmost extent of the village and directly linked with Town Gate before Foulridge was bisected by the new Skipton Road.

TRENT
The area on Skipton Old Road which grew around Trent Farm. The name seems to mean 'trespasser' and is generally used in the context of a river liable to flood. Trent Well still flows freely and it seems the farm took its name from the spring of which 'strongly flooding' may well have been an appropriate description.

TUGG'S CLOSE
Former name of the land 'to the east of the road from Foulridge to Colne' on which Close House was built.

VILLAGE
Earlier name for the Town Gate area, the centre of the village.

WALLER HILL
Reputedly named after the wallers who built the canal embankment. Once a small community. The 1851 Census recorded 21 separate households still residing here.

Warehouse Lane.
Photo by Thomas Robinson.

WAREHOUSE LANE

Warehouse Lane was built by the Canal Company and was a busy thoroughfare between the village and the warehouse on Foulrridge Wharf. By the 1940s the Procters had moved from No. 40 to No. 1 Station Road, Ernest Ingham had the grocers on the corner of Abner Row, and the Colne Co-operatice Society ran the premises at 10 Warehouse Lane.

WEETS

A corruption of wet? The whole of the moor is a sponge full of water for most of the year.

WESLEYAN FIELD

A field off Reedymoor Lane where the Wesleyans held sport days, picnics and the like.

WHITEMOOR

Described in 1581 as '*The waste called Whyt Moor*'. Various meanings have been suggested:
- White having the meaning 'high ground'
- White - land covered with bent grass
- a corruption of 'Weet Moor'.

Chapter 6

LORE AND LEGEND

Various traditions have arisen out of attempts to explain the origin of place names and it is sometimes difficult to extract the fact from the fiction.

Civil War traditions

There are a number of stories about Oliver Cromwell's association with the village. Most are interesting, some amusing, but few have any factual foundation.

The tradition that Oliver Cromwell gave **Foulridge** its name by exclaiming "*What a foul ridge*" is pure fiction. It is doubtful that Cromwell even came to the district. Documented spellings of the village's name go back to the early 13th century (400 years before Cromwell). Curiously the spelling of the name did undergo a change during the Civil War period from '*Folrig*' to '*Fowlerigge*', and by 1650 had assumed almost its present form being then spelt '*Foulrigg*'. This may well account for the tale.

A similar story claims that an exclamation from Cromwell's wife "*What an admirable gell*" led nearby Admergill to be so named. Again this is romantic fiction.

The tradition that Cromwell Street takes its name from **Cromwell's Croft** on which it was built does however seem to be based on fact. We know from contemporary sources that Parliamentarian troops were garrisoned at Emmot Lane Head in 1643 to check the Yorkshire cavaliers, and the following year saw a skirmish at Colne. Foulridge, in common with most of the district, overwhelmingly supported Cromwell during the Civil War and the village had its own Roundhead officer, Major William Barcroft of Noyna, and it is quite likely that Cromwell's troops were billeted in the croft.

Two rather romantic traditions attached to **the Foulridge or Tailor's Cross** also date to the Civil War period. The most popular tells of a Royalist tailor who refused to make uniforms for Cromwell's troops. The story tells that the obstinate, loyal hearted tailor was shot and the stone placed over his remains had scissors carved on it as a warning to his fellow 'snips'. The crude carving on the cross resembling a pair a shears is more likely to be pincers, one of the instruments of our Lord's passion. The cross is a medieval preaching cross and its name is probably a corruption of Tal-lers after the Knights Hospitallers who held land at nearby Alkincoats.

A differing legend gives rise to its alternative name, the **Maiden's Cross**. It tells of young Margaret Burnard who waited beside the cross for her lover, Robert, to return from the Civil War. He died at the battle of Marston Moor but Margaret refused to accept his death and returned each evening to their meeting place. Following an incident with some Royalist soldiers Margaret was apparently killed

The Tailor's Cross.

and her body buried at the spot where she had so often waited in vain.

A certain amount of fact seems to be interwoven with fiction in this tradition which tells of Robert's brother, William, breaking the news of his death to Margaret. It may be a coincidence but, at the alleged period of the incident, there was a Margaret Burnard living at Alkincoats, who became the second wife of William Barcroft.

A number of farms on the Kelbrook border contain the word '**Hague**' in their title and several quite plausible stories have been put forward to explain how the name originated. One is that when the surrounding marshland, known locally as 'The Bottoms', was being drained Dutch workmen were employed on the project and were billeted in the area causing it to be renamed after the capital of Holland. Another explanation is that the name came from the low fever or 'ague' which prevailed near the marshland prior to the drainage. The area was not in fact drained until the 1820s and references to the name Hague date back to 1381 so, although far less appealing than the Dutch connection, it is far more likely that the name has the same origin as the various *Heys* near County Brook, being originally '*a place surrounded by a hedge*'.

Witchcraft

Fear of witchcraft persisted in the district long after the notorious Pendle Witch trials of the early 17th century. Our ancestors were extremely superstitious and used various charms to ward off evil spirits. A written charm, found at Daubers c.1929, and known variously as the Daubers or **Foulridge Charm**, has been

The Daubers or Foulridge Charm.

authenticated by the British Museum as probably dating to the 17th century. It translates after three lines of apparent gibberish as follows:-

"*As it is said in the 17th chapter of St Matthew, at the 20th verse, By faith ye shall remove mountains, may it be according to faith. If it be, or shall be that …. any demon resides in or disturbs this person or place or this beast, I adjure thee in the name of the Father, the Son and the Holy Ghost to depart without any disturbance, trouble or tumult what so ever. So be it.*" Then follows the Lord's Prayer.

Tales of the Supernatural

Over the years there have been many reports of strange occurrences in and around Foulridge, probably the best known are the **Hobstones hauntings**.

The name of this old farm alone points to a sinister association, '*Hob*' being a Saxon word for hobgoblin, an evil dwarf or devil. The building has a history of hauntings and poltergeist activity – violent knockings in the night, bottles hurled through the air, broken windows, moving furniture and frightful apparitions of a monk brandishing the bloody stump of a severed arm. Peter Wightman recounted the story of the spectre in his book 'Pennine Panorama'. The tormented monk was seen in 1959 by one of the occupants while sat on an outside privy. (How vulnerable can you get?) This led people to suggest that there may have been some religious house on the site and that the spirit who would not lay itself to rest had been the subject of religious persecution.

Hobstones.

Standing Stone Gate Farm.
Photo by Peter Wightman.

There were monastic sites at nearby Admergill, Barnside and Gill, but there is no evidence of any monastic building at Hobstones or of any gruesome event, but terrifying happenings in the 1970s convinced the then occupants that the house was besieged by demons and, in a state of near hysteria, they contacted the Rector of Colne, Noel Hawthorne. Aided by an exorcist from the Fylde coast, he drove the evil spirits away. Hob was finally ousted.

Pubs seem to have been a popular haunt for ghosts. **Standing Stone Gate Farm**, at the junction of the Barnoldswick Road with the roads to Blacko and Foulridge was built in 1791 and served originally as a wayside inn for travellers on their way from Settle to Colne and Burnley. The story lingers of families living there being woken in the night by the sound of coach and horses, the screeching of brakes, loud voices and urgent banging on the door.

The **Hole in the Wall** boasted the ghost of an old horse dealer who used to plague the pub of an evening. His ghost dates back to a time when an old barn, now demolished, used to stand adjacent to the inn. One night the horseman's favourite horse died and the heart-broken man died the following day. The barn was later apparently used as a mortuary and former landlady, Nora Shaw, said "*I saw his apparition and it terrified me. I refused to sit up at night afterwards. It was a grey, ghostly shape of a body of a man, although it had no bodily substance.*" Other people experienced a bad atmosphere but when the stables were demolished in 1960 the atmosphere changed and the ghost was never seen again.

The **New Inn** has the dubious distinction of being the most haunted pub in Pendle. The inn has a ghost believed to be connected with a Cavalier who died in conflict in the neighbourhood. Others claim it was connected with the nearby Quaker burial ground. During the 1960s a number of renovations were carried out at the inn and successive landlords were troubled with footsteps during the night, followed by mysterious knockings on the bedroom door. Some years earlier a small bedroom at the rear of the inn was affected by a large luminous cross which would form on the ceiling even when the curtains were drawn and the room was in total darkness.

The Barnside Murder

Not surprisingly some ghost stories are associated with gruesome events in the vicinity. One of the district's most famous murders occurred at Barnside in 1789 when a girl named **Hannah Corbridge** went for a Sunday morning walk with her 'accepted lover' Christopher Hartley. A week later she was found in a ditch, poisoned and with her throat cut. Hartley was committed to Lancaster, convicted and executed, and for years there were stories of Hannah's ghost being seen in the Barnside area. According to her burial entry in the Colne Parish Register she was '*big with child*' with her throat '*cut so deep that her head only hung by two teguments behind*'.

Spooky times at Pauline and Des's bed and breakfast ...

IT was three o'clock in the morning when the man staying at the picturesque 16th century farmhouse was awakened by a strange rattling noise.

He sat up in bed and stared at the door. By the light of the moon through the window he could see the old metal sneck moving frantically up and down, as if someone was trying to take it off the latch and open the door.

The man's heart missed a beat as he recalled the words of the lady of the house: "Don't worry if you hear strange noises. It'll be George the ghost."

GHOSTLY GOINGS-ON? Pauline Connolly (right) with husband Des and best friend Joan outside Reedymoor Farm, top right.

Ghostly happenings at Reedymoor Farm in the 1980s and 90s.

Chapter 7

LEEDS AND LIVERPOOL CANAL

In the mid-eighteenth century the idea of linking Leeds and Liverpool by water caught the imagination of businessmen as part of the nation's canal building boom. The prospectus for the canal was published in 1769 by John Hustler and an Act of Parliament was passed the following year. Construction began in 1770 simultaneously on both sides of the Pennines. By 1777 the canal was open between Liverpool and Wigan and between Leeds and Skipton, but crossing the Pennines posed greater engineering problems and it was almost twenty years before the local part of the Lancashire route was finally agreed on.

The coming of the canal dramatically changed the appearance of the valley bottom and had a profound effect on village life. Work started locally in the late 1780s when an army of 'navvies' descended on the district to cut the giant inland navigation line, and build with the simplest tools the locks, bridges, tunnel and reservoirs. The work spanned several decades and shanty towns grew up at Reedymoor, Waller Hill and along the canal banks to accommodate the men.

Shanty town reconstruction.

Above: The Foulridge Tunnel is sometimes referred to as *the hole in the wall* as this is how it appears from the Foulridge end.

Above right: The Marton Emperor at County Brook.

Robert Whitworth designed the **Foulridge Tunnel** and proved to be a first class engineer, if a remarkably poor prophet *"I will find it necessary to lay the land level 33 feet below the summit at Foulridge Lane and to carry the canal for about 1,500 yards in a tunnel underground. This tunnel .... will be a small affair..."* In the event the Tunnel took five years to complete at a cost of £40,000, and was the most expensive single item on the entire canal building project. Soft soil made tunnelling impossible and only 700 yards were actually dug underground; the rest was constructed on the 'cut and cover' method involving digging out from the top and later arching over and covering by earth to keep the sides firm.

The tunnel is one of the most impressive engineering feats of the Georgian age. It was a hazardous undertaking, but life was cheap, the navvies expendable. Many of the stones lining the tunnel weigh over a hundredweight and were manhandled into place. Scores perished in the task. Forgotten and far from home some were unceremoniously buried beneath the canal banks where they had died. Hardly surprisingly the men were a rough, troublesome brood, much given to drinking, brawling and poaching and utterly contemptuous of the heavily outnumbered constables and gamekeepers who opposed them.

Date of Baptism	Date of Birth	Surname	Child	Father	Mother	Father's Occupation	Residence
16.11.94	27. 5.94	Lund	Jonas	Henry	Jane	Hatter	Stone trough
5. 8.04	16. 2.04	Lund	Luke	Thomas	Betty	Hatter	Heir law
25. 6.10	30. 1.98	Lund	Mark	Henry	Jane	Hatter	Cragg
30.12.92	29.11.92	Lund	Mary	Joseph	Elisabeth	Black Smith	Barrowford
3. 7.08	23. 3.08	Lund	Mary	William	Grace	Inn Keeper	Colne
16. 6.11	7.11.10	Lund	Richard	Thomas	Betty	Hatter	Hatflaw
6.11.96	11.10.96	Lund	Sarah	Henry	Jane	Hatter	Stonetrough
12. 5.05	10. 3.05	Lund	Sarah		Jane	Hatter	Now
23. 6.93	17. 6.92	Lund	Susanna	Henry	Jane	Hatter	Stonetrough
17.12.04	27.12.04	Lund	William	William	Grace	Inn Keeper	Colne
3.12.09	20. 9.09	Lund	William	Robert	Ann	Hatter	Foulridge
19. 6.98	10. 2.96	Mackenzie	Alexander	Alexander	Mary	Canal cutter	Oldham
19. 1.00	23.12.99	Mackenzie	Daniel	Alexander	Mary	Navigator	Burnley
6. 9.07	7. 3.07	Mackenzie	David	Alexander	Mary	Miner	Rushton
3. 2.05	1.11.04	Mackenzie	John	Alexander	Mary	Navigator	Henfield
2. 1.03	5. 4.02	Mackenzie	Margaret	Alexander	Mary	Navigator	Henfield
7. 1.98	12.12.97	Mackenzie	Sarah	Alexander	Mary	Navigator	L. Marsden
3. 4.09	25.12.08	Mackenzie	Thomas	Alexander	Mary	Labourer	Altham
8. 1.92	4.12.91	McHoys / McKuoys	Margaret	John	Mary	Canal cutter / Navigator	Barrowford
5. 1.96	16.11.95	Markenick / Muckinick	Hugh	Hugh	Ann	Labourer	Todmorden
10. 6.98	11.11.97	McKeswick	Mary	Hugh	Ann	Navigator	Waterside
29. 9.93	6. 9.93	McKeswick / McKenrick	Martha	Hugh	Nancy	Laborer	Foulridge
25.12.01	24.12.01		Martha	Hugh	Ann	Navigator	Colne
6. 4.94	20. 3.94	Makenzie	William	Alexander	Mary	Labourer / Canal cutter	L. Marsden Chapel
24. 6.92	30. 5.92	McClim / McClim	Henry	Henry	Margaret	Labourer	Wanless Water
6. 9.95	10.10.94	Maugh	Ann	Henry	Margaret	Navigator / Cannall cutter	High fold Hay
29. 4.07	22. 3.07	Marklend	Betty Hartley	John	Betty	Gentleman	Crag
20. 7.06	30. 4.06	Manley	Ann	Oates	Peggy	Mason	Bradley
24. 7.00	6. 4.06	Manley	David	John	Mary	Weaver	Barrowford
20. 6.00		Manley	Elisabeth	James	Elisabeth		Pasture
15.12.11	8.11	Manley	Elisabeth	John	Mary	Weaver	Barrowford

– 133 –

Colne Parish Church Baptism Register entries 1790–1812

Robert Whitworth, the chief engineer of the Canal Company, brought down to Lancashire many of the men who had been working with him on the Forth and Clyde. Among these was Alexander MacKenzie, born at Muirton in 1769. He worked as a canal cutter firstly in the Colne district and moved westward as the canal was built. In the early 1790s he married Mary Austin at Colne Parish Church and eight of their eleven children were later christened there.

The 8-mile Burnley / Foulridge stretch of the canal, which included the tunnel and wharf, was completed in 1796 and the Official Opening celebrations lasted four days. Canal Company shareholders and their guests sailed through the new subterranean wonder on a fleet of boats to the accompaniment of a military band and a volley of cannon; and a splendid Ball was held at the Colne Cloth Hall.

The canal changed the pattern of local life in a few decades. It brought jobs to the village. New occupations – lock keepers, leggers, wharfingers, warehousemen and boatmen – came into being, and existing tradesmen such as quarrymen, masons, smiths and carpenters benefited. The canal provided an impetus for trade. Whereas raw material and finished goods had previously been transported on the backs on packhorses, suddenly there were barges able to carry comparatively enormous loads at a fraction of the cost. Heavy machinery, coal and building materials could now be easily transported. The Canal Company had agents in all the principal towns in Lancashire and Yorkshire. Fleets were operated by carriers, colliery companies and others. The Canal Company's own fly boats plied to Gargrave, Skipton, Bingley and Leeds, and regular packet boats connected with all the main towns on the canal, a fast service of light vessels drawn by two horses, with first and second class cabins, heating and refreshments.

With no towpath in the tunnel, the tow-horses were unharnessed at one end and walked along Reedymoor Lane whilst the boats were 'legged' through the dank depths. Small buildings at either of the tunnel provided stabling and were used by professional leggers waiting to provide their services to boatmen who would shout "*Legger Ahoy*". Leggers became so proficient that they could get a loaded boat over the 1,640 yards distance in an hour and an unloaded boat in half an hour. Legging ceased in the early 1880s after the death of a legger by suffocation and the introduction of the Foulridge Tunnel Steam Tug.

As a boy during WWI Tom Draper was allowed to leave school prematurely to help his father at the tiller of the tug in the vital task of ferrying through war supplies. The tug at times worked both day and night, pulling as many as 13 boats behind it. It was fitted with propellers and a rudder at each end so it did not have

Above left: This photograph taken in the Foulridge Tunnel in the 1930s demonstrates how leggers worked. The men laid on boards at either side of the vessel and pushed with their legs against the tunnel walls, literally walking the barges through.

Above right: The Foulridge Tunnel Steam Tug.

to turn round. In winter she was often used as an icebreaker.

The steam tug operated until 1937 when diesel-engined craft succeeded, controlled by tunnel keepers using a telephone, and from 1957 until 1963 by traffic lights operating on a time switch. Pleasure craft using the tunnel then had to ensure that passage was clear before entering. Traffic lights were subsequently reintroduced.

Unlike many canals the Leeds & Liverpool was very prosperous. Its shareholders received dividends continuously from 1786 to 1919. The peak years, between 1843 and 1846, paid 34%. It stood up to the competition of the railways far better than any other canal and played an important part in both world wars. Today its use has changed to become recreational. It is still navigable throughout its 127 miles and passes through scenery of great natural beauty as well as interesting relics of the industrial revolution.

Bob Booth designed and commissioned the canal cruiser the '*Marton Emperor*' in 1981 and founded **Foulridge Leisure Cruises**. Originally based near Barrowford locks, he moved to Foulridge wharf where the family lived. His most prestigious passenger was the Prince of Wales in 1986, and the subsequent owner, ex Royal Navy diver Kevin Rollins piped the Prince aboard in 1988. The boat was purchased by Martin Cleaver in 1993. He welcomed the Prince on his third trip on the Emperor in 2008 and continues to operate Foulridge Canal Cruises from the old wharf.

Foulridge Wharf

The wharf was completed by 1796 in time for the Official Opening of the Foulridge Tunnel. The warehouse was built in 1815, a year before the canal opened in its entirety. In the heyday of the canal the wharf bustled with boats loading and unloading their cargoes. Raw cotton from America arrived here from Liverpool to supply the local mills.

Beside the warehouse was the wharf master's cottage, which also housed the office and stables where barge horses could be exchanged or rested. The white metal pillar between the warehouse and bridge is the base of a crane which used to lift goods off the barges onto horse drawn carts.

The railway bridge overhead once carried the Colne/Skipton line and was the only mainline railway crossing the canal in Pendle. Apparently the ground was so marshy here that the foundation piles had to be sunk to the same depth beneath the ground as above.

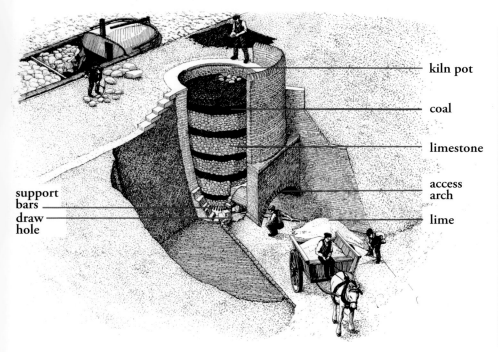

kiln pot

coal

limestone

access arch

lime

support bars

draw hole

In 1989 an interesting piece of industrial archaeology took place on the wharf when the old lime kiln was restored. The kiln probably dates to the early 1790s when the local section of the canal was constructed and enormous quantities of lime were required to make the mortar for the locks, wharf, bridges, tunnel and the clay lining for the bottom of the canal. In the early days, the limestone came from Lothersdale by 'Lime Gals' (Galloway ponies) via Black Lane Ends. When the kiln was in use, 200 tons of wood kindling, coal and limestone were loaded

Above left: A cutaway drawing of the lime kiln in use.

Above right: The old Lime Kiln.

The Foulridge Cow

In 1912 a cow named Buttercup fell into the canal at the Barrowford end of the tunnel and swam through to the other end and into the annals of Foulridge. The exhausted swimmer was revived with alcohol, and a photograph in the nearby Hole in the Wall pub recorded the incident. The caption with the picture stated "This cow owned by Mr R Brown, Blue Slate Farm, swam the full length of the Foulridge Mile Tunnel, September 24th 1912".

'Old Ebby'

Old Ebby's real name was John Pollard. He had a reputation for sticking to old fashions and wearing knee breeches in vogue in an earlier generation.

In his early days he acted as an errand boy for the men who were repairing the Foulridge Tunnel and in later life he took the farm at Slipper Hill and looked after the reservoir there.

He died in 1892 aged 81, and is interred at Salterforth.

Slipper Hill Reservoir, known as 'Old Ebby's'.

Frank and Julie Mallalieu outside Foulridge Tearooms, 2000

by hand, and after slowly burning for days, produced 50 tons of lime. During the excavation a wide range of objects was discovered, including clay pipes, glass bottles, part of an old Volkswagen and the remains of a dead donkey.

In the early 1980s Bob Booth renovated the derelict canal cottage to create a shop and tearoom. More recently the Foulridge Tearooms were run by Frank and Julie Mallalieu but closed in September 2003 as a result of British Waterways refusal to renew the lease.

The sell-off of the wharf buildings by British Waterways in early 2000s caused a period of uncertainty after the Borough Council's unsuccessful bid to buy them failed, but the wharf has since been given a facelift with the restoration of the Canal House and Canal Cottage by the Berry family, and the refurbishment by the Randell family of the Warehouse which opened as Café Cargo in August 2009.

The Leeds and Liverpool Canal

- is the country's longest canal with a total length of 127 miles
- took 46 years to build
- opened in 1816 and links the seaport of Liverpool with the Aire and Calder Navigation at Leeds forming a through route between the Irish Sea and the North Sea
- the summit of the Leeds & Liverpool Canal is at Foulridge and the canal is fed from the various reservoirs in the area

Foulridge Reservoirs

A few facts and figures

Foulridge Lower Reservoir
now commonly known as 'Burwains' is the largest. Constructed in 1793, and deepened in 1832, it covers an area of approximately 108 acres and its greatest depth is 33 feet. Capacity 373,000,000 gallons. Originally known simply as Foulridge Reservoir, then the 'Large' Res. It became known as the 'Lower' Res when the 'Higher' Res was constructed in the 1860s.

Slipper Hill Reservoir
covers about 13 acres with a greatest depth of 28 feet. It is more commonly known locally as Old Ebby's after the man who farmed Slipper Hill Farm and looked after the reservoir at the end of the 1800s. The name appears as the 'Little' reservoir on the Tithe Award map of 1842 and also as the postal address for The Boat House, Slipper Hill in 1910.

Whitemoor Reservoir
was built in 1840 adding a further 150 million gallons capacity. Unlike the other canal reservoirs, in times of drought, water from natural springs on the hillside of Whitemoor are used to augment the Colne water supply to Foulridge.

Foulridge Upper Reservoir
was formerly known as Carr's Res after the Carr family of Langroyd who owned the land on which it was constructed, and had the boating and fishing rights. It was also known as the 'New' Reservoir as it was not constructed until 1865, more than 70 years after Foulridge Lower Reservoir. In the 1900s it was simply referred to as the 'Middle' reservoir.

Brown Hill Reservoir may not appear on any official map but the name is used locally to refer to the flooded field to the east of Foulridge Upper Reservoir, also constructed in the mid 1860s. Brown Hill Lane is not built on a dam but a causeway providing access to farms, so both sides are actually Foulridge Upper Reservoir.

Chapter 8

ROAD AND RAIL

Standing Stone Gate, at the junction of the Barnoldswick Road with the roads to Blacko, Colne and Foulridge, takes its name from the standing stone sited close by which acted as a signpost for early travellers. It is referred to as 'the standing stone on Harrock Hill' on the 1581 Map of Whitemoor.

Ancient Roads

A Survey of Highways of 1623 refers to '*Churchbridge in Foulridge Lane to the waye meeting forth of King Yate*' indicating that Foulridge Lane ran southwards via Kirk Bridge towards Colne. **King Gate**, now the site of the Langroyd roundabout, was an important intersection in medieval times where Foulridge Lane joined the main road to Colne (via Windy Bank) and linked with Red Lane, and Back Lane (now Castle Road) to Yorkshire. It was known as King Gate because Red Lane was the beginning of the King's Highway to the manorial castle at Clitheroe.

Foulridge Lane (now part of Skipton New Road) divided near the present site of the Hare & Hounds – one road to Barnoldswick, via Cocker Hill and Standing Stone Gate, linked with the Bracewell road to Gisburn and Settle; whilst the other road followed the line of Skipton Old Road via the Cragg, Accornley and the Hague to Kelbrook.

Burwains Lane ran from Waller Hill through the old Burwains Estate, and across the water meadows to join up with Red Lane prior to the valley being flooded by the reservoir. **Reedymoor Lane** and **Smithy Lane** (more commonly known as Shirt Neck Harry) were part of another ancient road leading to Colne. These lanes became particularly important during the construction of the Leeds & Liverpool Canal when wagons trundled incessantly from the Red Lane quarries with stone for the reservoir embankment and the Foulridge Tunnel.

The Turnpike Road

Until the early 1800s the main form of transport for most people was by horse or on foot. Some wealthy folk had their own carriages but the roads in the area were generally poor. There was no direct link to Skipton by a low valley road. The highland route via Lidgett and Black Lane Ends over Elslack Moor was only really suitable for packhorses and individual travellers; for coach and horses the route would have been impossible because of the steep gradients of the hill.

The 'New' Skipton Road was built by **the Colne & Broughton Trust** and was the last turnpike road to be built in the district. The Act of Parliament for the Colne & Broughton Trust was given royal assent in 1824 and gave trustees power to build the road and construct gates where tolls could be charged. The original trustees included many owners of land through which the new road passed – the most notable being the Tempests of Broughton, Kayes of Thornton, Parkers of Alkincoats and Carrs of Langroyd. Some trustees were early cotton manufacturers and included Nicholas England, who ran St Helen's Mill at Colne Waterside, Thomas Thornber of Vivary Bridge Mill, and John Hartley of Carry Bridge.

Once known as **Dyson's New Way**, the road's construction provided work for unemployed handloom weavers at a time of great distress. The road was originally intended to start opposite Carry Lane Head but the trustees were unable to obtain the farmer's permission so the route was altered – hence the curve in the line of the road towards Skipton Road top in Colne.

There were two toll houses and gates, known as 'bars', erected along the line of the road – one at Foulridge, the other at Thornton. Both were built in 1827 but no trace of either remains. The Foulridge Toll House stood immediately opposite the entrance to St Michael & All Angels Church causing the adjacent stream to be renamed **Bar Beck**. The turnpike road brought an increase in wheeled transport – carters transported goods to and from the canal wharf to onward destinations, and by the mid 1820s were daily stagecoach services with names like the '*Telegraph*' and '*Invincible*' rattling through the village providing regular passenger transport between Colne and Manchester, Preston, Skipton, Keighley and Leeds. These coach services virtually disappeared when the railway line to Colne was completed.

The development of canal and railway transportation led to toll roads becoming increasingly unpopular and charges were finally abolished in the 1870s. The Foulridge Bar was pulled down in 1875/6 and the Toll House was demolished shortly after. The last toll bar keeper was Turner Snowden who combined his job with other occupations. In the 1851 Census he was listed as a weaver and is later described as a tailor.

A hundred years after the making of the Colne & Broughton road, history repeated itself when the 'New Road' to Barnoldswick was constructed in the early 1930s to provide work for the unemployed. Cycling superseded horse transport but was not without danger. Two separate accidents in 1936 reported the victims suffering from concussion and shock.

Turnpike milepost

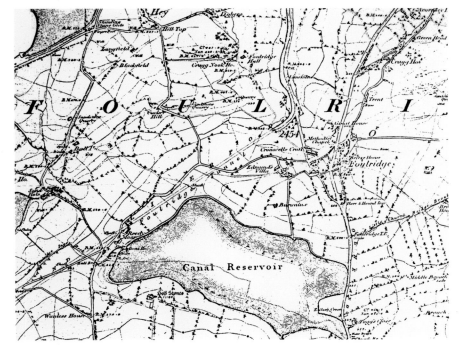

Detail from the 1847 Ordnance Survey Map of Foulridge, the first 6" to the mile map of the village. It shows Edmund's Villa, below which is a completely blank space except for the road leading to the station. The terraced houses on Station Road and Peel Mill are conspicuous by their absence, not yet having been built. The land on which Springfield was built is marked as Blackfield, Daubers is spelt Dobers, and Bar Beck is still referred to as Little Church Bridge Brook.

Wilson Tinniswood, the last Foulridge station master.

The Railway

The railway arrived in the 1840s. The Midland line from Skipton reached Colne in October 1848 and the following February the East Lancashire Line, later the Lancashire & Yorkshire, joined it to provide the Lancashire connections. By the 1920s the line had become the London, Midland and Scottish (LMS).

In its heyday the 11 1/2 miles between Colne and Skipton carried freight and long range passenger services, as well as local trains. For more than a hundred years Foulridge station was busy with travellers eager to spend the day shopping or on a day trip out to the Yorkshire Dales and, not long before the sweeping cuts to the railways were made, grand steam trains including the famous Flying Scotsman could regularly be seen speeding through the village. The station even boasted a goods yard of sorts with several sidings.

Trains have not run through the village since 1970 when the Colne/Skipton line closed. Foulridge station closed some eleven years earlier in January 1959 and, after standing derelict for many years, it was given a new lease of life when it was dismantled stone by stone and transported across the Pennines to Ingrow on the Keighley & Worth Valley Railway where it was reconstructed. The official reopening of 'Foulridge' station took place in March 1989.

Foulridge station in the late 1800s.

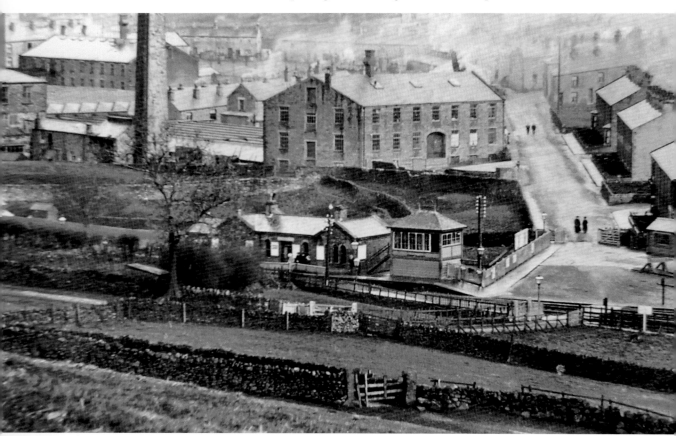

Colne-Earby Pioneer bus, 1906 was the first motor bus service to run through Foulridge. It was owned by three Colne businessmen who were the innkeepers of the Commercial and Union Hotels, and Mr Mitton who later developed a sizeable transport undertaking.

Early Buses

Fifty years after the coming of the railway, witnessed the arrival of the first buses. The earliest ones were horse-drawn. Locally there was a horse drawn charabanc which used to ply between Earby and Colne, mainly at weekends. This was superseded in 1906 by the first motor bus service inaugurated by the Colne and Earby Motor Omnibus Company from the Swan Hotel in Colne. The bus, named 'The Pioneer' was a 4-cylinder 30 h.p. Crossley Leyland, but the vehicle does not seem to have been outstandingly reliable and passengers preferred to travel by rail, leading to the bus suffering an early demise.

Ezra Laycock probably the best known independent operator of all, later ran a service through the village. In 1921 Colne Corporation obtained powers to run omnibuses and purchased four second-hand Tillings-Stevens petrol-electric buses and a service between Colne and Earby, via Foulridge and Kelbrook, started operating in January 1923. The buses were, however, underpowered and were taken out of service.

Public transport was taking over and competition for routes became keener. Colne Corporation pursued an aggressive policy to eliminate competition which led to various disputes between Laycock & Son and Colne Corporation in the late 1920s with innumerable Laycock route applications and licences being refused.

Laycock & Sons instituted an Earby-Klondyke-Salterforth-Barnoldswick service on Christmas Eve 1929, and a Barnoldswick-Salterforth-Colne service was also introduced, but this was withdrawn in favour of an extension of the Earby route to Colne soon after, because of competition from the Ribble route between Colne and Barnoldswick via Standing Stone Gate and the poor road surface between Salterforth and Kelbrook.

The decline in passenger numbers after 1950 saw a gradual reduction in services. BC&N became Burnley & Pendle JT when the new Pendle Council was created in 1974. The 1980s saw the demise of the service from Colne to Barnoldswick 'over the tops' via Hill Top and Tubber Hill. In 1996 the two local authorities sold their shareholdings to Stagecoach UK and, for the first time in almost 100 years, the local council was not directly involved in providing a public transport service. Despite these changes, Foulridge still has a regular and reasonably priced bus service linking the village with its near neighbours and enabling people to travel to all corners of the UK.

The By-Pass is passed by ...

The arrival of the M65 in Colne in 1988 led to increasing pressure to build a Colne/Foulridge By-pass along the former railway line to help divert motorway traffic from North Valley Road into Yorkshire. A debate raged with villagers being divided between rival 'Build our By-Pass' and 'Scrap the By-Pass' campaigns but, even when the By-Pass was approved, possible start dates were continually deferred for more than two decades and the project has been shelved because of financial constrictions. Residents are now coming to terms with the fact that the long-awaited By Pass may not be built at all. In 2009 Lord Greaves said "*the original scheme for a road is now by the wayside*".

.... but will the Railway return?

In recent years SELRAP (the Skipton–East Lancashire Rail Action Partnership) has campaigned to bring back the railway and re-open the line between Colne and Skipton reconnecting Pennine Lancashire with both Manchester and Leeds. Many argue that this trans-Pennine route should never have closed. Massive increases in road congestion and the issue of global warming have also put reinstatement of the line on the political agenda and the prospect of seeing trains cross the county boundary in Pendle now seems both achievable and increasingly likely. The undue hasty removal of the Foulridge canal bridge angered many at the time, but it now seems unlikely it would have been used again, and the cost of rebuilding is dwarfed by the biggest obstacle - an underground tunnel beneath Vivary Way in Colne.

British Rail is currently (2009) selling off the track bed for £50,000 and Lancashire County Council has been urged to buy the land between Colne and the former county boundary near New Hague at Kelbrook. The former track is continuous from Vivary Way, Colne apart from the missing bridge over the canal at Foulridge.

Traffic congestion through Foulridge continues to increase and shows little sign of improving in the foreseeable future. One wonders at the final outcome. In the meantime the railway track is a temporary bridleway / cycleway/ footpath.

Let's create an airport

On a lighter note, is it really possible that Foulridge may have its own airport? In 2007 Graham Cannon requested permission from the Parish Council for occasional hot air balloon flights to take off from the recreation ground. Permission was granted.

Press cutting from the Colne Times, 12 October 2007.

■ **Flyers want to use sports ground**

Let's create an airport!

TAKE OFF: The hot air balloon used by village residents. (S)

SUGGESTIONS of an airport in the village came as some what of a surprise to Foulridge parish councillors at the latest meeting.

Coun. Graham Cannon, of Cocker Hill, Foulridge, who is the joint owner of a hot air balloon, is set to ask councillors at the November meeting for permission to take off from the sports ground in Foulridge.

Coun. Cannon, a civil engineer, is training to be a pilot and hopes to qualify soon. He owns half of the balloon and the other half is owned by Peter Haworth, a qualified pilot who also lives in the village.

The pair, who have permission to take off from the Stirk House Hotel, Gisburn, are fully insured and follow advice from the National Farmers' Union and the County Landowners' Association.

Both are members of the British Balloon and Airship Club and follow its code of conduct.

"We tend not to fly very often and we're always cautious not to disturb stock.

"I think hot air balloons create interest from a lot of people who would consider it an interesting thing to have in the village. We've seen how successful the Festival of Flight in Barlick has become.

"We'd probably not fly it very often and never if the ground was being used for football games or was wanted for any other reason. It sometimes gets too boggy up there as well so we wouldn't bother going up there then," said Coun. Cannon. He added that if he was approved permission, he would also be prepared to take people up in the balloon.

"The fantastic views you get when you're up in the balloon really are wonderful," he added.

The parish council is to discuss the proposition on Monday, November 5th. Meetings are at Foulridge Village Hall at 7-15 p.m.

Chapter 9

TEXTILES AND OTHER TRADES

The Wool Trade

A damp climate and heavy soil led to the early development of a domestic textile industry locally to supplement the meagre income from a smallholding. A fulling mill had been erected at Colne Waterside by 1296, and during the following centuries sheep rearing became important and the woollen trade grew.

Ambrose Barcroft of Noyna was a wool merchant and recorded sending packhorses to Lincolnshire to bring back wool on a fairly large scale. 24 June 1691 *"Richard Boothman went ... this day to buy wool for me ... £150."* On the 30th Lawrence Spencer followed with two horses and 15 pack cloths in which to bring it back. All through the summer he was sending for and receiving wool. Meanwhile the spinning continued: April 1691 *"I weighed 37 copps of warp yarns that is in a basket wch was spun by the lasses and it is 7 1/2 lbs".* *20 April 1691 "4 1/2 lbs of dighted (cleaned) weft fleece wooll I intend to sell to Jo Atkinson who will give me as much weft skein wool for it."*

During the 17th and 18th centuries clothiers and others connected with the textile trade built new houses in stone, a sign of prosperity. Ball House and Hobstones are two of several houses rebuilt by yeoman engaged in the wool trade.

At the top of Ball House Lane was this **Bargain Stone** – where the touch of a hand became as good as a receipt. The custom began when farmers assembled around the stone to strike a bargain for the cattle or wool they had. When the price was agreed, they sealed the bargain by touching hands through the hole in the stone. The stone was damaged by farm vehicles in 1998 and was subsequently removed to the garden at Ball House.

After fulling, cloth was crumpled and needed to be straightened and dried under tension. This was done on **tenter frames**, often up to 45 yards long. The sites where these frames were erected can be identified from old field names. There was a tenter field at Hobstones. The expression 'on tenter hooks' derives from this method of drying.

The **Colne Cloth (or Piece) Hall** opened in 1775. The lower storey was used as a storeroom, while the upper floor was the sale room fitted out with 190 stalls; the entrance being at the top of the flight of steps.

Most of Foulridge's population was engaged in carding, spinning, weaving, tenting and dyeing. Some handloom weavers obtained their warp and weft from clothiers who operated the '*putting-out system*' and paid weavers on receipt of the finished cloth. A small number of master weavers became employers of labour and built dandy shops, the earliest form of factory, where workers lived on the lower floors and worked at the handlooms on the top storey characteristically fitted with long rows of windows to the front and rear in order to admit the maximum amount of light. The Quaker Meeting House in Ivegate became the *Foulridge Dandy Shop*.

By the second half of the 18th century Colne was the centre of the woollen industry in NE Lancashire and the Cloth Hall was built in 1775. In 1781 Foulridge was producing almost 3,000 pieces of worsted annually.

Industrial Revolution

The physical appearance of the village altered at the beginning of the 19th century. The canal transformed the valley-bottom; large areas of low-lying ground were flooded for reservoirs whilst others were reclaimed by drainage schemes; a turnpike road dissected the old village, and dry-stone walls appeared on the hillsides as the common fields were enclosed. It was a period of great change. The population increased steadily from 833 in 1801 to 1458 in 1841, mainly brought about by work generated by the building of the canal.

Foulridge appears to have escaped the unrest and chartist riots which affected Colne. Much of the distress was caused by the cotton trade depression but, as the 1851 Census shows, woollen handloom weaving was still the village's main occupation long after neighbouring Colne and Trawden had moved onto cotton and power looms.

The fall in Foulridge's population between 1841 and 1851 may have been due to the fact that new mills being built in Colne, Nelson and Barnoldswick were gradually beginning to draw labour away from the village.

King Cotton

The first cotton mill in the village was **Peel Mill**, sited on land between Station Road and Warehouse Lane. Originally known simply as Foulridge Mill, it was built in 1855 by the Foulridge Mill Building Company, as a small cotton spinning mill and leased to **Watson and Richard Bracewell** of Colne who later converted the mill to weaving. Water for steam power was obtained from the nearby Leeds & Liverpool Canal, and a tunnel leading from the canal was used to manhandle coal by means of wheelbarrows from barges to the boiler house.

Even after Foulridge got its own mill, hand and power looms coexisted for some time. Many local people were reluctant to exchange working in their cottages and relative independence for the factory system. They were fortunate in that they had become skilled in manufacturing *mousseline-de-laine* (a lightweight fabric made from fine worsted yarn) and for a time work was plentiful and wages were good. The 1851 Census shows that the principal occupation in the village was handloom weaver 'delaine' with family members, mainly young children, acting as bobbin winders. Gradually however the handloom was discarded by all except those who were too old to work in the mill.

By 1869, in addition to Bracewells, other manufacturers of cotton and worsted mixture goods in the village included Robert Foulds at *County Brook Mill*, and Marshall Sellers at *Midge Hole*. The National School logbook also refers to several 'half-time' children being admitted from **Croft Mill** in the 1860s. This was not the present Croft Mill but an earlier one housed in premises which had previously been the *Foulridge Dandy Shop*. It closed in 1874 when the owner, Alfred Howe, a cotton spinner and manufacturer from Manchester, sold the premises which then became the *Foulridge Brewery*.

In 1882 the weaving shed at Foulridge Mill was extended and a two-storey warehouse built facing Station Road. The building of New Shed led Foulridge Mill to be called **Peel Mill**.

New Shed opened in December 1891. The **Foulridge New Shed Company** was formed in 1890 under the name Foulridge Room & Power Co. Ltd. The room and power system allowed small shareholders to invest in the building of mills, the Shed companies acting as landlords for a multiple-occupancy of firms. The building of the mill contributed to a dramatic increase in the village's population between 1891 and 1901, and the village grew to accommodate the new workforce. Rows of terraced houses were built to provide housing for the millworkers and shops sprang up to cater for them.

The Mills on County Brook

There were originally three water-powered mills on the County Brook; Wood End, Midge Hole and 'New' Mill. All pre-dated the Leeds & Liverpool Canal. Originally known as Black Brook, the County Brook stream formed the old county boundary between Lancashire and Yorkshire, and supplied the motive power for the mills.

The first mill at County Brook was **Wood End corn mill**, which was in existence by the late 1600s. It was built by John Pollard and, judging from Thomas Barcroft's letter written in 1694, it was a thriving concern as, unlike the Foulridge Mill, it had a good water supply and its own drying kiln (a big advantage in a damp climate like the Pennines). By 1810 Wood End Mill is described as '*ruins*'. It was sited just above County Brook Mill, above the footbridge across the brook.

In the clough just downstream from the Mount Pleasant Chapel is the skeletal form of **Midge Hoil Mill** which probably derived its dialectal name from its diminutive size. The mill was powered by a water wheel and would originally have been a spinning mill putting out yarn to handloom weavers in their cottages.

The mill dated to around 1790, and surprisingly survived the impact of the construction of the Whitemoor Reservoir which affected the flow of the County Brook, and by 1868 it had become a small weaving shed run by Marshall Sellers. Following his untimely death from a chill, he was succeeded by his brother, Ezra, who ran the mill as a power loom mill with 24 looms making winceyette shirting. By 1882 Ezra found it impossible to carry on as the Canal Company's new waterman wanted too much '*palm oil*' (i.e. bribe) to let the water down from the reservoir to suit the working of the mill, and he transferred the business to Nelson and later to Chorley.

William Yates in front of the Midge Hole Mill.

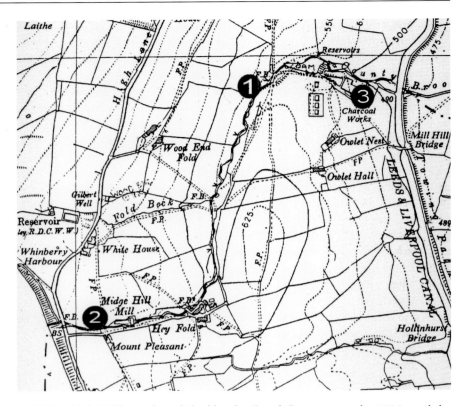

Detail of 1894 6" OS Map showing location of the Wood End Mill, Midge Hole & County Brook Mill. The latter two are marked as 'Midge Hill Mill' and Charcoal works; Wood End Mill was sited between the two.

Midge Hole Mill was demolished by the Canal Company in the 1890s and the stone reused for repairs. The outline of the mill dam and a depression, which at one time would have housed a water wheel, can be identified about a hundred yards below the old Chapel on the opposite side of the stream.

County Brook Mill was the third of the water mills to be built at County Brook and was the last mill in the district to be driven by water wheel. Built about 1750 'New' Mill started life as a corn mill and has had various uses over the years. The mill has also had several names including Hey Mill, 'Stew' Mill and County Brook Mill.

In the early 19th century Messrs **Yates & Riley** started a mordant dye works in a portion of the site, now taken up by a small area of the present weaving shed. It was here that wood was 'stewed' resulting in the local name of '**Stew**' Mill. The residue from the chemical making for the dyeing trade was of course charcoal.

The dyestuff was transported to Broadoaks Dyeworks in Accrington and to the Lowerhouse Mills. The carter was a Mr Capstick who lived in the cottage underneath Mount Pleasant Chapel. County Brook Lane was deeply rutted and it took two horses to pull a lorry load of two barrels to the top. The horses knew the route so well that on the return journey Capstick, who liked a drink, could call at the Hare & Hounds, fall asleep on the lorry and the horses would take him safely home. After the partnership was dissolved Yates carried on, and then his wife, Sarah and their son William ran the business. In 1928 when the site was being cleared to make way for the first section of the weaving shed, some of the retorts were still in existence and underground tanks containing liquor were found. These were quickly emptied by the local farmers who used the contents as a form of creosote on their hen huts and other wood outbuildings.

By April 1877 the name had become County Brook Mill and was being used as a weaving mill by a William Sagar. In 1907 the mill was taken over by William Mitchell and the association with **the Mitchell family** continues to this day. William and his family lived in a cottage attached to the mill. His two sons, Ernest and Norman, followed him into the business and from small beginnings they gradually expanded. Four successive weaving shed extensions between 1927 and 1936 increased loom capacity from 50 to 400. As the family grew, the living accommodation became too small and they built three houses above the mill for William and his sons, Ernest and Norman.

Ernest's two sons, Raymond and Neville, continued the business. Now they have been followed by Raymond's sons Adrian and Lance.

Mitchell Interflex is Lancashire's oldest working cotton mill and the only mill still weaving in Foulridge today. Most of the products until the 1940s were interlinings for men's suits. Today, tie linings, deck chair fabrics and many other types of cloth are woven for a wide export market.

The mill was powered by a water wheel supplemented by the steam engine until the 1950s. By the end of the decade the shed was electrified and it became uneconomic to use the original power. The wheel was demolished in 1960 and the shaft can be seen in the mill yard.

County Brook Mill.

Berry's (Croft Mill) Coronation 1953.

The Twentieth Century

Foulridge mills thrived in the early 20th century. Ernie Macro, retired secretary of the Colne Weavers' Union, remembered the village during the 'forties and 'fifties *"When all the mills were running full-time, Foulridge was really busy. All the mills finished work at the same time, and the number of buses in the village taking workers to Colne and Earby had to be seen to be believed"*.

In 1897 **Lonsdales** took over at Peel Mill and ran it for 60 years, broken only by a period during the last World War when it was taken over as a food storage depot. 1957 witnessed the end of textile activity when the mill was sold to **Armabord**, manufacturers of plastic bathroom accessories. When the firm closed in 1982 the future of the mill was secured by being taken over by Weston Electrical Units.

Between 1905 and 1906 **New Shed** was doubled in size with weaving shed extensions being erected in the direction of Warehouse Lane. Over the years the mill became the home of a number of firms including **Messrs. Threlfall, Roberts and Hopkinson**. Roberts' entrance was from Low Well, Hopkinsons from Warehouse Lane. By 1925 J F & H Roberts had become the mill's sole operator, running looms in the mill for 30 years until about 1960.

The present **Croft Mill**, built in 1922 by **Joseph Hargreaves**, was originally known as *Great* Croft Mill and later as *New* Croft Mill. The firm failed financially and the mill was taken over by **Wm N Berry & Son** of Earby in the 1930s who brought a number of workers to live in Foulridge. Still affectionately referred to as **Berry's mill**, it employed many villagers and operated until 1969. The mill subsequently had a rather chequered history with a number of firms having space, including Earby Light Engineering, Bradley Textiles and J W Coates & Co. Kanda Hepple arrived in 1978, and for the past 30 years has operated **Croft Mill Shop** providing textiles via retail, wholesale and mail-order. More recently **Colne Carpets** have occupied part of the mill.

Apart from County Brook Mill the weaving looms have long been silent, and recent years have seen the loss of various employers including Mal Tool Engineering, Armabord, and in 2008 Lakeside Garden Centre and the removal of Causeway Glass to Colne, but a number of small one-man businesses have sprung up. The 2001 Census listed 103 people working 'mainly at or from home',

Ted Fort in the early 1970s near the old Fort Vale Engineering works on Norfolk Street, Colne. Fort Vale has won three Queen's Awards for Exports.

Interestingly World War II benefitted the village as far as employment was concerned. As well as the mills being in full production making fabric for service uniforms, it brought a long-term benefit to the area with the establishment of engineering firms supplying the aircraft industry. It began in neighbouring Barnoldswick when Rolls Royce acquired the Rover car plant in 1943 and a 'shadow industry' developed in military automotive production. As well as Rolls Royce providing jobs for hundreds of local folk, it led to new engineering firms being established to supply components for RB aero engines. It also had wider, less obvious, local ramifications such as **Ted Fort** of Lancashire Ghyll, destined to be a painter/decorator, obtaining an apprenticeship at Rolls and going on to found Fort Vale Engineering, world leaders in the supply of specialist valves and obtaining an OBE for his services to industry.

In 2010 Foulridge still has precision engineering firms supplying the aerospace industry. The first engineering firm in the village was **Weston Electrical Units**.

Westons's Peel Mill Building.

The founder, Richard Sutton, was chauffeur/gardener to the Sir Amos Nelson family in the 1920s and gained his early engineering expertise in that capacity. He set up business at St John's Garage in Nelson in 1929, and a few years later he came up with the electro-mechanical invention which was to revolutionise betting on the Tote. This was the prototype of the electronic wizardry which today controls Tote odds throughout the country in a split second and was arguably the first electrical computer ever to be invented.

Though reasonably successful with his garage business, Richard Sutton realized in 1936 that he did not have the kind of money to launch his invention. He approached his former employer, Pemberton Nelson, who brought in his brother-in-law Bert West, and they put up the money in return for the patent of Richard's idea. The three men entered a partnership and when it came to choosing a name for the company they put the syllables of each of their names into a hat and decided to abide by the first two drawn out. The 'Wes' in Bert West's name was first out, then the 'ton' in Richard Sutton's and Westons was born. The revolutionary electronic calculator went up on most dog tracks in the north of England before Westons switched to munitions during the war. At the end of hostilities Richard Sutton had enough capital to start up entirely on his own as Weston Electrics.

When Geoffrey Sutton was awarded the MBE in 1995 he modestly remarked "It's for us all – a tribute to my family and the work force."

Weston EU has been Foulridge's main employer for more than half a century. Founded in 1948, Richard and Doris Sutton were succeeded by their son, Geoffrey, who subsequently received the MBE for his service to industry. Weston is still owned entirely by the Sutton family, now run by Geoffrey's sons, Richard and Jim. Belying an ultra modern production environment run to Japanese Gemba Kalzen principles, an unmistakable and friendly 'family' atmosphere pervades the organisation.

Weston EU is one of the most technologically advanced engineering companies in Europe, and a world leader in aerospace technology. For over 35 years the company focused on the production of airframe components, then with the advent of new technology in the mid-1980s it expanded into the IT sector. The ensuing years have seen them serve yet more diverse markets and today Weston supplies a wide spectrum of high technology products.

In the 1980s Weston acquired the empty Peel Mill and made a multi-million pound investment in its conversion. The blend of heritage and high-tech typifies Weston and its premises; the original buildings have been skilfully restored for offices which lead back to purpose-built 'state of the art' manufacturing units.

Weston Group staff outside Peel Mill 1992. Weston EU currently (2010) employs 280 split between Foulridge and the West Craven facility 4 miles away.

The company has grown progressively and currently operates from two sites in the UK comprising 120,000 sq ft floor space, located in Foulridge and a new West Craven facility at Earby. The group also has a wholly owned subsidiary company, Weston SEA, which is located in Thailand.

Other Foulridge engineering firms include **T & R Precision Engineering** in Lowther Lane, contractors to the Civil and Military aircraft industry specialising in precision multi axis machining of components, and **Pendle Polymer Engineering** in Warehouse Lane, founded in 1981 to supply rubber mouldings and fluid seals to the automotive and industrial sectors. As well as utilising the whole range of polymers, PPE has years of experience in working with rubber to solve engineering problems.

Hat-making

As well as handloom weaving and spinning, felt hat-making was a flourishing cottage industry in Foulridge in the 18th and 19th centuries. The Colne Parish Baptism Register for 1790-1812 refers to no fewer than 52 hatters residing in the village with a further 17 just outside the boundary.

As with other domestic hatters in Lancashire it is likely that the locally produced hats were coarse felt and that the trade consisted in the main of producing felt bodies which were sold locally and sent to either Manchester or London to be finished. Rabbit fur and wool were the principal ingredients with the boiled bones being used as an adhesive.

Mercury was often used in the moulding process to prepare the fur for felting, and hatters risked mercuric poisoning causing madness, hence the expression 'mad as a hatter'.

A number of place names such as Hatters Bridge and Hatchet Lane remain as a reminder that hat-making took place in the locality.

In the 1960s stone moulds for felt hat-making were found at **Cragg Nook**, suggesting that this was once a hatmaker's cottage. At the rear of the building are external stone steps which once led to a workshop above – a single large room which ran the full length of the upper storey.

Although now badly eroded, the moulds clearly show the type of hat produced – the 'tricorn' worn by the middle class and the flattish 'round' hat for the better off working class. Once the hats had been shrunk and felted they were shaped on such moulds, dried and dyed.

Blacksmithing

Matt and Willie Bulcock
outside the Foulridge Smithy,
1950s.
Photo by Thomas Robinson.

The Bulcocks' hardware/
ironmongers shop at end of
Belmont Terrace. An Advert
for William Bulcock in the
Church Magazine of the 1930s
described him as *Shoeing and
Jobbing Smith and General
Ironmonger*.
Photo by Thomas Robinson.

*My sledge and hammer lie reclin'd
My bellows, too, have lost their wind,
My fire's extinct, my forge decayed,
And in the dust my vice is laid,
My coal is spent, my iron's gone,
My nails are drove, my work is done.*

Source: Foulridge Blacksmith's grave, Colne Parish Church

Horses were not only the main form of transport, but also the main beast of burden used for ploughing, carting and towing barges along the canal, and blacksmithing was a vital occupation from early times.

In 1665 Great House Farm was occupied by '*James Robinson of Foulrigge, Blacksmith*' and deeds refer to the smithy there. On 22 January 1690 Ambrose Barcroft wrote '*Jonathan Robinson shod me 4 oxen and 2 of my sons*' and in November 1690 he recorded buying 2 cwt of iron '*for ironing a pair of wheels.*'

The village smithy at the rear of the Hare & Hounds inn was in existence by 1824 and was used by coaches using the new Colne & Broughton turnpike road. The stables served passing stagecoaches including the '*Telegraph*' and '*Invincible*' which rattled through the village providing regular passenger transport.

The **Bulcocks** were village blacksmiths for more than sixty years. William Bulcock Snr served his apprenticeship at Bolton Hall in Bolton-by-Bowland, which in 1894 kept 70 horses with grooms, stable lads and blacksmiths. By 1895 he was established at the Hare and Hounds smithy. In the early days, three forges operated with six men often working from 5 o'clock in the morning until 11 o'clock at night. By 1914 both William's sons, Willie and Matt, had joined the family firm. The Bulcocks lived at 12 Skipton Old Road beside the smithy and later moved to 45 Belmont Terrace where they also ran a hardware shop.

The smithy remained in use until the late 1950s, the last smithies being Willie and Matt Bulcock. Matt lived above the family ironmonger's shop at the end of Belmont Terrace, but Willie moved to Trawden. Smithing had its perks because after shoeing the horses he used to take the manure home on the tram for his roses, no doubt to chagrin of his fellow passengers. In its latter years the smithy engaged in all types of metal work – mending tools, welding etc for farmers, builders and manufacturers.

Quarrying

Foulridge stands almost entirely on millstone grit and, hardly surprisingly, there was a large stone quarry on Noyna where millstones were quarried from medieval times. The millstones were roughly cut until circular, and then rolled down the hill for further dressing. Flagstones and wallstones were also quarried at Noyna End, and Red Lane quarries provided stone in the 1790s for the Burwains reservoir embankment and other canal works during the construction of the Leeds & Liverpool Canal.

Noyna Quarry (also known as **Wilk's Delph**) provided stone for building local cottages, mills, bridges and field walls. A narrow gauge railway ran down the hill from the quarry to meet the canal in the valley bottom.

By 1840 **Robert Ridehalgh** of Breeze House was both '*Farmer of 22 acres and Quarry Master, employing 8 labourers*'. **George Sagar**, described variously as quarry master and stone & flag merchant, ran the quarry from the 1870s and during the late 19th century the quarry provided stone for rows of terraced houses in the village. **George Ormerod**, also one time quarry master, and builder, built Ormerod Terrace, Chapel Street and Parkinson Street.

Noyna Quarry closed in the early 1900s, but Foulridge maintained a link with quarrying. The **Law Hill Quarry** (beside Colne Golf Club) produced more than 50 huge grindstones a year used in paper pulping in Norway and Canada and the stones were carried one at a time by horse drawn carts to the canal at Foulridge to be taken to Liverpool for shipment. The quarry closed in 1939.

This old row of cottages at Trent is shown on the 1843 Ordnance Survey map. The two 3-storey cottages were probably weavers' cottages and the smaller ones seem to have been built later, probably for or by the quarrymen working at the quarry. There are traces of tracks leading down from the quarry to Trent Row.

Chapter 10

HISTORIC HOUSES

Chester Kneller with
grandchildren at the back of
Accornlee late 1990s.

No trace of either of the former Barcroft houses remains other than the farmhouses – Foulridge Hall Farm and Noyna Hall Farm, but a number of 17th century houses have survived. Some of these were built by lesser gentry, yeoman farmers who became wealthy by their involvement in the wool trade.

Accornlee / Accornley (1611)

is a Grade II listed building and undoubtedly the finest example of 17th century vernacular architecture in the village. The house was originally associated with the **Acronley** family who lived there until the mid 1600s. The name was both a surname and place name and was spelt variously. The place is referred to as early as 1259, then spelt Akerlandeleye, when an inquiry was made into the transfer of land to Geoffrey the Harper by Adam de Acornley who was afterwards hanged. Peter Wightman rather tongue in cheek commented "*perhaps an acquaintance with a harper preceding employment as such*"!

In the Hearth Tax of 1666 Accornlee ranked as the largest house in Foulridge. It was then the home of the **Smith** family who lived there for over 150 years. They were succeeded by the **Fort** family, and at the end of the 19th century it

Accornlee, 1939
Accornlee is a large H-plan
house of two storeys, with
centre porch, large gabled wings
and attic. The main facades are
symmetrical and a dripstone
extends all around the building.
The house also has multiple
fenestration – Chester Kneller
recalled painting 98 windows!

was one of several farms bought by **Edward Carr** so that he could build a private coach road to his Shooting Box on Kelbrook Moor. During the latter half of the 19th century the farm was tenanted by the Greenwood family, followed by James Veevers, and since the early 20th century by the **Kneller family** who subsequently purchased the property from the Carr Estate.

A fire at Accornlee in 1928, created by newly gathered hay spontaneously combusting, caused devastating damage to the barn and destroyed the 1611 date stone.

In 1968 the farm was used in a scene in the filming of 'The Tenant of Wildfell Hall' and for a few moments Jean Kneller became a film star and received the princely sum of £5. In the mid 1980s Chester Kneller uncovered a splendid old inglenook fireplace with beehive ovens on either side.

Breeze House

Tucked away behind the high wall opposite the New Inn stands Breeze House, one of the oldest houses in the village. Reputedly dating to 1619, the house was probably built by the **Holgates**, a prominent local family who lived there during the 17th and 18th centuries.

Elizabeth Shackleton of Alkincoats recorded that the **Foulridge Bull Baits** were held here during the 1770s when the house was occupied by John and Robert Holgate, two bachelor brothers who led the lives of country gentlemen, hunting and fishing with the local gentry.

In one of the garden walls are two rectangular open-faced recesses known as **bee-boles** made to shelter the old straw hives or 'skeps' in which bees were formerly kept. Honey was used as a sweetener when sugar was an expensive and rare commodity. Beeswax was also expensive and in constant demand.

At one time large quantities of grain were grown in the district but, as the growing season was short, it was necessary to dry the corn in purpose-built kilns where charcoal or peat fires beneath the floor heated the damp corn which was spread on perforated tiles. Stone floor joists or **rackstones** supported the floor. There are a number of rackstones scattered around the garden at Breeze House, two being incorporated into garden steps. The stones were originally part of the floor of a corn-drying kiln sited nearby.

The **Ridehalgh** family acquired Breeze House in the early 1800s. The estate included Noyna Quarry and by 1840 **Robert Ridehalgh** was described as '*Farmer of 22 acres and Quarry Master, employing 8 labourers*'. In the early 1870s, by then '*an old gentleman*', he was responsible for starting Foulridge Church at Breeze House along with his daughters, Miss Renny of Burwains and Miss Wood from the Cragg.

On Robert Ridehalgh's death in 1874, Breeze House was purchased by **James Whitaker** 'the Elder' who not only farmed the land but also worked full time at the local mill as a tackler, or weavers' overlooker. He died in 1895.

Breeze House Farm was situated on the east side of Skipton Old Road adjoining Breeze House. Following the death of Alice Whitaker in 1907, the estate was put up for sale by auction at the Crown Hotel in Colne and was purchased by **Henry Hewitt-Dean** of Kirk Rise. The most southerly portion of Breeze House Farm,

Alice Whitaker sitting in field at Breeze House c.1900 James's wife, Alice smoked a long clay pipe and according to family tradition is reputed to have said "that there was bother wi' brass and bother 'bout it, but she preferred to have bother we' it". Hence her husband's two jobs!

Two-seater privy
In the garden of Breeze House were several outbuildings including a small one-up, one-down cottage for a farmhand or groom (demolished in 1956), a stable and a double-seated lavatory. The two-seater privy is probably the only one surviving in Foulridge today.

This is the front of Breeze House with its long range of mullioned and transomed windows, and continuous dripstone running between floors. The Grade II Listed Building was one of only three buildings in Foulridge included in Pevsner's 'North Lancashire'.

Pendle View 1911 Coronation Year H.P.

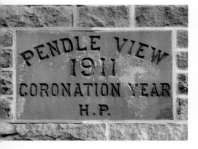

known as 'Low Meadow', was sold to Henry Priestly who built Pendle View. His initials appear on the date stone.

Rennie Croasdale bought Breeze House in 1911 and the family lived there until the early 1980s. The farm was tenanted by **Abner Brunskill Barritt** for almost 40 years. There was no farmhouse and he lived at the Hare & Hounds, where his wife sold beer and ran the inn, which led to the farm being often referred to as '**Hare & Hounds**'. Abner moved to Ormerod Terrace c.1928 and worked at Great House Farm, but continued to farm at Breeze House until at least the late 1930s.

Breeze Farm barn was known as '**The Joanna**' or '**Joanna Chapel**' after Joanna Southcott, the infamous religious fanatic, whose followers used a small room over the stable approached by outside stone steps in the early 1800s. A hundred year later men came over from Ireland for hay time and slept there. Burnley RDC acquired the land in the 1950s and demolished the Barn to build Breeze Close Flats.

Gradually the farm land was eroded as several plots of land were sold off as '*excellent building sites*' to be subsequently developed. A few acres here and there became used for free range poultry until the 1950s when the land was compulsorily purchased by Burnley RDC. Highfield Avenue was named after 'High Meadow' on which the firstly the council houses and later the two rows of old people's bungalows were built.

Ball House

The porch at Ball House bears the inscription '*IM 1627 AM*', the initials of the builder, **John Moore** 'gentleman' and his wife Ann; 'I' in those days was interchangeable with 'J'. Part of the building however was standing much earlier, a '*Bawlhous*' on the same site being recorded on the **map of Whitemoor of 1581**. In the latter years of the 17th century Ball House was the home of another **John Moore, the celebrated blind Quaker preacher**, who was imprisoned in Lancaster Castle for refusing to swear an oath.

Stone seats inside the porch bear a number of shallow depressions caused by sandstone being crushed to make sand for spreading on the house floor. The house also has various features connected with the wool trade including a blocked up doorway on the first floor where bales of wool or cloth were stored, and a lant trough in which urine was collected because of its ammonia content for cleaning wool.

Early in the 18th century Ball House passed into the hand of **the Waltons** (a branch of the Marsden Hall family) and from 1710 Francis Walton and his descendants were to occupy the house for more than a hundred and fifty years. It was during their occupation that chaos came to the valley in the form of the construction of the Leeds & Liverpool Canal. One of the last of the family to live at the house was James Walton, or **Jem o' Ball** as he was known, who gained a reputation for terrorizing the district making every highway in the vicinity unsafe for innocent travellers. He was a notorious 'strong arm man' employed as a debt collector, repeatedly fined and in and out of gaol for assault. On one occasion he visited the Crown Hotel in Colne in pursuit of a non-payer, seized the unfortunate victim and sat him on the fire until he promised to pay. For this escapade Jem was fined £20. He certainly enlivened the neighbourhood. A far cry from Quaker John Moore, but then '*it takes all sorts!*'

In 1968 the house featured in the BBC television production of Anne Bronte's classic '**The Tenant of Wildfell Hall**'. The house has another Bronte connection – there is an oriel window built into the gable end which came from the porch of **Wycoller Hall**, the Ferndean Manor of Jane Eyre.

Below left: Front of Ball House.

Below right: The oriel window from the porch from Wycoller Hall was rebuilt into a new side entrance in the early 1970s by Roland Halstead.
The porch had been at Trawden since 1855 when it was bought by David Bannister to provide extra rooms for his family of eleven children; Ralph the youngest was the father of Sir Roger Bannister, the first man to run a mile under four minutes.

Sand Hall.

Sand Hall

1606 Sandall	1708 Sand Hoall	1843 Sand Hole

The name derives from the sand deposits left by the glaciers, being originally the site of a sand pit. This small sand quarry was used in the construction of nearby Slipper Hill Reservoir. Throughout the 18th and 19th centuries the name was spelt Sand **Hole**, but the earliest reference in the Colne Parish Registers on 7 February 1606 records the baptism of '*Maria, daughter of Christopher Smythe of Sandall.*' A century later the baptism of '*Ann, daughter of John Emmott of Sand Hoall*' appears, suggesting perhaps a transitionary spelling between hall and hole, so the name may well have been Sand Hall originally.

The present house was certainly there in the early 1700s and **a** house was there a hundred years before. The 1851 Census lists James Widdop, aged 50, farmer of 12 acres, his wife Mary and six children. Over the centuries occupants have included the Emmotts 'of Foulridge', Wilkinsons, Halsteads, and John Robinson described as '*butcher, Towngate & farmer, Sandholes*' in the 1920s. The property was still a farm until 1978 when it was purchased by Ashley Holt.

Moss Houses

Off Watery Lane, about 1/2 mile south-east of Noyna, is Moss Houses which dates to the second quarter of the 17th century, and was owned by **the Bolton family** for almost four centuries. Thomas Bolton, who was living there in 1670, was described as a '*clothier*', and in 1681 Henry Bolton '*of Mossehouse, Yeoman*' was one of only 16 persons in Foulridge who had lands of a yearly value of £4. The Bolton family was quite important locally and their property included Higgin House at Colne and Hague House at Kelbrook. In the 19th century members of the family lived at Emmott Hall and Leach House in Colne.

Luke Cryer farmed Moss Houses in the late 1800s, succeeded by Robert Dixon in the early 20th century.

The name Moss Houses refers not only to the house but to a small hamlet comprising a number of separate properties. The Tithe Award Map of 1842 shows a cluster of properties, and the 1851 Census lists 9 separate properties with no fewer than 50 people living there. In some cases families were simply tenants and not owners, and it is consequently often difficult to establish with certainty which family occupied which property.

Hollybush Farm.

Hollybush (Moss House)

Near Slipper Hill Reservoir is Hollybush Farm, formerly called **Moss House**, and referred to variously as *Moss and Foulridge Moss*. The name was changed by Mr & Mrs Jim Taylor in the early 1960s because of the constant confusion with Moss Houses on Noyna; in fact the Taylors had only been there a few days when milking equipment destined for Moss Houses was delivered to them by mistake. The new name 'Hollybush' came from the profusion of holly in the vicinity.

Moss House was the home of a branch of the **Mancknowls family of Townhouse** in Nelson in the early 1600s. The family had been one of Marsden's wealthiest but lost much of its fortune during the Reformation by adhering to the

Catholic faith. The Moss House branch subsequently took up residence at Cragg in Foulridge and the Mancknowls pedigree shows that Moss House descended to the Wilsons.

The house bears a date stone of **James and Ellen Wilson 1725** but architectural features suggest the building dates to the late 1600s. Moss House and Heyroyd in Colne were both owned by Thomas Driver in 1524 and a link between the two properties was maintained for more than 250 years – James Wilson's son rebuilt Heyroyd in 1777. The Wilsons came from Cowling and became substantial landowners locally; in addition to Heyroyd they owned nearby Knaze Edge and property at Bents, then known as Upper Colne.

The Taylors moved to Moss House in 1958. Jim Taylor was the Borough Engineer for Colne from 1949 until his retirement in 1973, before the creation of Pendle Council. His wife, Ena, was a manager of St Michael & All Angels School and was associated with numerous local charities and organizations including Dr Barnado's, Lifeboat, Cancer Research, Colne Dramatic Society and Colne & District Local History Society. The couple frequently provided refreshments for history society walks around the village.

Hobstones

The building which dominates the hillside overlooking Burwains Reservoir is a fascinating one, a farm called **Hobstones**. In its heyday it was an important house with traditional links to Alkincoats, which stood just across the summit of the hill to the south.

The name is interesting, 'Hob' being a Saxon name for dancing elf or fairy as in Hobgoblin, although some maintain the name is derived from *Devil's Stones* and the building certainly has a history of haunting. One resident witnessed the appearance of a maimed monk and occupants in the 1970s were driven to have the house exorcised.

Hobstones was built by Edmund Stephenson who was a clothier.

Silver flagon presented to Dr John Turner in 1775.

Hobstones has various connections with the area's once thriving textile industry. The present house built by **Edmund Stephenson**, a wealthy yeoman clothier, bears three date stones: 1700 above the doorway, '*ES 1704 IS*' above the curious gateway (the initials of Edmund and Jenet Stephenson), and 1710 on the later right-hand wing built as a specialised workshop.

When Edmund Stephenson died in 1715 his inventory shows he had a great deal of wool and cloth including combed worsted, spun worsted and wool yarn, a hot press, a cold press, five handlooms and a number of warps in the hands of outworkers. Obviously he practised the putting-out system.

There had been an earlier house on the site – in 1513 Hobstones was held by the **Hargreaves** family, and soon afterwards it was acquired by the **Parkers of Alkincoats**. Alexander Parker of Hobbeystones was a clothier in 1574. **Edmund Waterhouse**, who lived there in the late 17th century, was also a clothmaker and the estate included a '*tenter field*' signifying a field where cloth was stretched out to bleach or dry. Restoration work in 1983 revealed several interesting internal features including well-worn steps which led to a loom shop in the upper rooms.

Perhaps the best known occupant was **Dr John Turner** who designed the Cloth or 'Piece' Hall in Colne in the 18th century. When the building opened in 1775 the proprietors presented him with a silver flagon which he subsequently gave to Colne Parish Church for Communion silver. Elizabeth Shackleton made a wedding visit to Hobstones in 1780 and wrote:-

'*My sone, his wife and myself all dressed and went in the chaise to make a wedding visit to Dr & Mrs Turner..... We were all entertained with wines, punch, ale, tea and coffee, and the ewer given to the Doctor by the proprietors of the Colne Piece Hall was converted into a coffee pot*'.

A century later Hobstones was occupied by the last headmaster of the ancient Grammar School in Colne – **Dr Halfhead**. He became discouraged because the wealthy sent their sons elsewhere to be educated and he was only getting the children of the poor tradesmen. He took to the bottle and, after a protracted drinking spree in the old White Horse in Colne, which resulted in the licence of that inn being suspended, Halfhead fell into disgrace. The Grammar School closed, and he retired back to Hobstones where his subsequent history is one of reappearances in court, unable to pay his rent, and even becoming involved in a bit of illicit whisky distilling.

More recently Hobstones has been associated with **the Bleasdale family** who farmed the land for generations. Michael Bleasdale was tenanting the farm in 1871 and the family purchased it from the Parkers in the late 1940s. The property has subsequently been split into several residences, but the Bleasdales remain at Hobstones to this day.

Burwains

The name Burwain is thought to originate from the OE '*byrgan*' meaning burial and suggests ancient occupation of the area. **Burwains House** was built by Dr John Turner of Hobstones in 1780, on the site of an earlier house. It was acquired by the Andertons in the early 1830s and subsequently extended. Occupation of the house alternated between the **Anderton** and **Renny** families, military men,

Burwains House

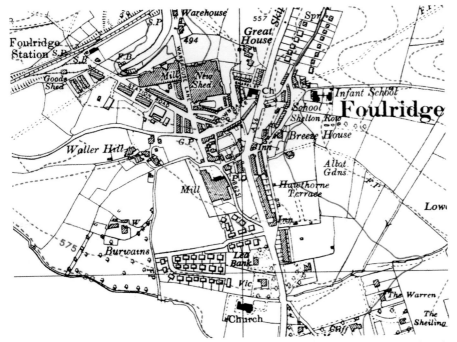

Detail of 1955 OS map showing the old Burwains estate prior to development. Burwains House stood in the centre of what is now the Burwains housing estate.

related to each other through marriage. A memorial in Colne Parish Church records that Major J W Renny, who fought in India, died in 1855 aged 44 on furlough. Captain John Anderton's tombstone at Christ Church, Colne records that he fought at Waterloo. Apparently he won his commission from the ranks, a very rare occurrence in those days.

In 1927 Burwains was bought by **Thomas S M Badgery** (known as Maxwell). Following his death the property was sold in 1954 to Major Royds, who in turn sold it in the 1960s to Kirks the builders. Kirks demolished the house and developed the modern Burwains housing estate.

Cragg

Cragg derives its name from the description of the landscape. An earlier house on the site was the home of the **Hartleys** during the 1500s, and later the **Mancknowls family** when they removed from Moss House.

A doorway at Cragg bears the inscription '1666'. When the New Skipton Road was being constructed in 1824 an underground tunnel was found, apparently connecting Foulridge Hall and Cragg House, perhaps dating to the time of religious persecution.

In 1837 **William Hewson Wood** inherited the house through his wife, Betty **Hartley** Mancknols, only child of John Mancknols, a solicitor. *'Mrs Wood, to the grief of her husband, died in 1843, aged, 36 and he did not marry again. He had two sons, who died in infancy, and a daughter Olivia, who always lived with her father and survived him.'* William Hewson Wood was the Chairman of the Colne Bench, and a Magistrate for 47 years. Before the Court House on Albert Road was built, he administered justice in many of Colne's inns including the old King's

Today Cragg is often referred to as 'the Pink House'
Its sudden transformation in the late 1980s came about following a Smith family holiday abroad where all the local houses were painted.

Head, the Red Lion and the Angel. He took an active part Foulridge affairs, and was involved in the erection and management of the National School and Foulridge Mill in the 1850s. He was perhaps best remembered for conducting the Sunday services at Foulridge School, and his life was sufficiently prolonged to see one of his most cherished dreams, the erection of a church in Foulridge, fairly set on foot.

The mounting block at Cragg is said to have been especially made for Magistrate Wood, who rode on horseback to the courts.

Mrs Cryer in her 'Memories of Colne' records a touching story of the devotion of an old servant when the family fell on hard times. She wrote: '*When things were at the worst this faithful old domestic came to her master and said "Don't you bother sir, they shan't have everything. I'll see to that". So when affairs were … settled, she took her master into the yard and, tipping over the swill tub, said "There sir what do you think of that?" And there lay all the valuable family plate, some of it heirlooms, bright and glittering in the sunshine, and good as new.*' W H Wood was generally respected and loved. On the day of his funeral every shop in Colne closed in respect, despite the fact it was market day.

19th and 20th Century Houses

Foulridge has a number of large houses which were built during the 19th and early 20th centuries. Those dating to the late 1800s include Springfield, Slipper Hill Boat House, Moorlands and Noyna Mede. Reef Edge was built in 1902, by the Pickles family who occupied a number of houses in the village including Reedymoor, Springfield and the Rock.

Many of the large houses on Skipton Road were also built in the early 1900s and were originally the homes of local manufacturers. These included Bankfield (James Roberts, of J F & H Roberts, New Shed), Eastfield (George Rushworth, Loom maker & Engineer), Burnside (Wm Berry, Croft Mill), and West Cliff (James Lonsdale, Lonsdale & Co, Peel Mill).

Springfield

Springfield dates to 1871, and was built on the site of Blackfield farm by Smith Smith of Netherheys in Colne for his brother Thomas Martin and sisters, Mercy and Ida. Tom Smith lived here for some fifty years from 1875 until his death in 1925.

The cottages now known as Springfield Cottages are referred to as '*Smith's Cottages*' on the 1912 OS map, and were occupied in 1901 by various estate workers including William Rushworth 'Gamekeeper', and Charles Harrison 'Coachman'.

Springfield was bought in 1925 by Sydney Pickles, a partner in the firm of Arthur Pickles and Sons, cotton manufacturers of Bankfield Mill, Colne. The next residents were the Nelson family (from 1949 to 1968) who were related to Sir Amos Nelson of Gledstone Hall. More recently the house was owned by Ian Skipper, whose father started selling pre-war Ford 8 cars from a wooden hut and expanded to become the well-known Skippers of Burnley, one of the country's largest Ford dealers. Ian Skipper latterly became well known for his association with the Jorvik Centre in York.

Springfield.

The Boat House, Slipper Hill

This was built in 1878 to house the Superintendent Engineer who was responsible for the supervision and maintenance of the five compensation reservoirs to serve the locks on this stretch of the Leeds & Liverpool Canal. It was also used as a shooting and fishing lodge for the Directors of the Canal Company.

With the rapid advance of road and rail transport, the canals gradually fell into decline and the house was sold to private tenants who, over the years, have included Samuel Bolton, succeeded by Geoff Le Gendre Bolton, Walmsley Riddiough and Fred Bannister (of Bannister Bros of Hollin Bank Mill, Brierfield) who lived there for 21 years until 1971.

Slipper Hill Boat House with reservoir in the foreground.

Moorlands

The site on which Moorlands was built was formerly known as Greenhead.

Described in 1879 as 'a pleasant mansion', the house was built by William Hallam, a descendant of the Waltons of Marsden Hall. Nearby Hallam Moor is a reminder of this connection. The house was subsequently tenanted by the Threlfall family, and in more recent times the house was owned by the Smith family who were connected with Smith's Tannery in Colne.

Noyna Mede

Noyna Mede was built in 1895 for William Argent Pilgrim, a highly respected local solicitor in the firm of Hartley, Pilgrim & Hayman (later Pilgrim & Badgery). Mr Pilgrim was a sidesman at Foulridge Church and for many years church garden parties were regularly held in the garden. Mrs Pilgrim was descended from the Barcrofts who had emigrated to Ireland, and Noyna Mede is said to have been so named after Noyna Hall. The Pilgrims retained the Irish link. In 1901 three of their four servants – the cook, housemaid and nurse - all came from Ireland, and throughout the 1920s and 30s they sent their laundry to Ireland, their horse-drawn buggy going each week to the station to collect it.

Noyna Mede.

Noyna Mede, 1960s.

In the 1950s Noyna Mede was purchased by the daughters of Jesus and became part of the Holy Rosary Convent. When the convent was acquired in 1978 to become the village school, the house was sold and reverted to a private dwelling. The property was later divided, one part being aptly named 'Pilgrims'.

The Close

The Close was built on land known as **Tuggs** which had been part of the Barcroft family estate in the 1600s. The original Close House was a small farm comprising roughly '*the land to the east of Dyson's Way* (Skipton New Road) *north from Kirk Bridge to opposite the church*'. The farm buildings with detached barn were on the opposite side of the road beside Croft Mill.

By 1851 **Barnard Crook**, the wealthy Colne draper featured in Robert Neill's book 'Mills of Colne', was living at Close House. Barnard owned much property and acted as agent for cotton growers in America. Considerable amounts of his cotton were brought up from Liverpool by canal and unloaded at the now derelict wharf at Wanless and brought into Colne by Blakey and Guy Syke (beside the Crown Hotel). Some of these deliveries were valued as much as £500. Barnard's death intestate in 1865, aged 84, at 'a house called Tuggs Close' led to a legal dispute. Three of his grandsons produced a 'purported' will in their own favour and took possession of the house and effects, all of which led in 1870 to a **Case in Chancery**.

The property was acquired by the Harrison family in 1874 and subsequently by William Argent Pilgrim. Close House was rented. By 1879 Edward Bird, brewery manager of the Croft Well Brewery was living there, and by 1895 the tenant was Thomas Hartley 'farmer and cart hirer'.

Robert Duckworth bought part of the farm nearest to Skipton Road in 1922 from Mr Pilgrim, demolished the farmhouse and built the present house. He ran the family preserves business in Colne and continued to own the Close until 1963 when it was sold to Alistair Baxter Cassie, Consultant Surgeon and subsequently to John Blair.

Below left: Dennis Mendoros OBE, DL, FRAeS was honoured by the Queen for his contribution to industry and is a Deputy Lieutenant.
In 2010 he was appointed High Sheriff for Lancashire.

Below right: Close House.

The present owner, **Dennis Mendoros**, head of Kelbrook aero-engine firm Euravia, was the founder of the Consortium of Lancashire Aerospace in the mid 1990s and its successor North West Aerospace Alliance.

Reef Edge

Reef Edge was formerly part of the Foulridge Hall Estate, the name suggesting some connection with 'Reeve', the local supervisor held responsible for the running of the Manor.

The house itself is relatively modern, being built by Arthur Pickles in 1902, and remaining in the family for 50 years before being bought by Roland Halstead. The house has been the home of John Bannister (of Duckworth's Chemist) since the 1980s.

Reef Edge.

Manor House

Originally known as **Kirk Rise**, Manor House was built by Colne Alderman, **Henry Hewitt-Dean** in 1912. In 1936 it became the home of another Colne Alderman **Edgar Duckworth JP**, who changed the name. Edgar was the son of Joshua Duckworth who built the first purpose-designed cinema in England – the Central Hall in Colne in 1907. Edgar was the Chief Warden of Civil Defence in Colne from 1939–1945. He sold Manor House to George Whittaker in 1947.

The house was subsequently the home of the Mayalls, followed by the Taylor family. Tom Taylor was MD of the Burnley firm of Diana Cowpe; his wife, Jean, founded Lakeside Garden Centre in the early 1970s which was sold to Mrs Ellis in 1990. Howard and Jean Rigg bought the house in 1991 and undertook a 2-year refurbishment.

Manor House was advertised in Lancashire Life in 2005 for £1.3 million (probably a Foulridge first) but in the event the Riggs chose to stay. When Lakeside Garden Centre closed at the beginning of 2008 it was acquired by Howard Rigg, bringing the land back under the same ownership.

Manor House.

The Duckworths

Three Duckworth brothers – Caleb, Joshua and Frances, born in Rimington in the mid 1800s, came to Colne in their teenage years and by the end of the century had established themselves as one of the most prominent families in the district.

Caleb (1854-1937) came to Colne in 1867 as an apprentice to Sir William Pickles Hartley (drysalter, grocer and jam manufacturer) and went on to found his own flourishing business, the Caleb Duckworth Jam Works in Colne Lane, and lived at the Ridge. His son, Robert, built The Close, and Arthur was a pharmacist and founded Duckworth's chemist shop in Albert Road.

Joshua (1856-1925) set up the printing works in Colne Lane in the 1880s. He was also a keen amateur photographer and in the 1890s began lantern slide lectures at the Cloth Hall. In 1907 he opened the Central Hall cinema in Colne Lane, reputedly the first purpose-designed cinema in England. Here he was able to show the new moving pictures to a spellbound Colne audience. His son, Edgar, lived at Kirk Rise.

Francis (1862-1941) was a wholesale grocer and had a shop in Foulridge in the 1920s at 47 Skipton Road (which later became the village Co-op). He became famous as a composer of hymn tunes, the best known being 'Rimington' which was sung by a massive congregation of British troops on the Mount of Olives after the surrender of Jerusalem during WWI.

Francis Duckworth's 'High-class Groceries and Provisions' shop boasted a Drapery department with a choice selection of ladies' and children's underwear etc. Arthur Barker was the resident manager.
Photo by Thomas Robinson.

The Ridge

With superb views over Burwains reservoir, the Ridge was originally occupied in the early 20th century by two Misses Riley followed by Caleb Duckworth until his death in 1937, Geoff Le Gendre Bolton (ex Boat House) and David Cunliffe, of Carrington Viyella, in the 1980s.

The Ridge.

Teneriffe Bungalow

This house was designed by Ernest Spivey for 'Barton' Turner Hartley, who was Mayor of Colne from 1910-1913. Originally known simply as 'The Bungalow', Turner Hartley changed its name following his honeymoon in Tenerife – but note the mason's misspelling of the name with a double 'f' carved into the front gatepost.

Turner Hartley was a cotton manufacturer who occupied premises at Oak Mill in Colne. During his mayoral term of office he witnessed a sorrowful procession make its way from Bethel Chapel on Burnley Road to Colne cemetery to bury Wallace Hartley, the heroic bandmaster of the Titanic. He also welcomed King George V & Queen Mary, the first record of Colne being honoured by the visit of a reigning monarch.

For years totally obscured from the road by trees, the bungalow and grounds underwent a complete refurbishment in 2004 by the present owners, Philip & Dorothy McIvor, founders of Farmhouse Biscuits.

Teneriffe bungalow.

Lea Bank

Next to the old Vicarage, Lea Bank was built by cotton manufacturer Joseph Hargreaves and named after his eldest daughter Selena, who assisted him in running 'New' Croft Mill, which he built. In the late 1920s Joe owned one of the village's first cars, a huge maroon open tourer Sunbeam, immaculately adorned with brass headlamps, horn and radiator. The mill lorry driver doubled as his uniformed chauffeur.

The house later became the home of George Wilmore, wine merchant of Church Street, Colne who was Mayor of Colne from 1949-50, and made a Freeman in 1962.

Lea Bank subsequently became the home of David Foulds, MD of the local firm E A Foulds (Lifts).

George Wilmore outside Lea Bank. Traditionally the Mayoral lamps were installed outside the Mayor's house during the Mayor-making ceremony.

Chapter 11

CHURCH AND CHAPEL

Early Religion

During the middle ages **Colne Parish Church** served the entire Chapelry of Colne which included Foulridge, Trawden, Barrowford and Great Marsden. Colne Church was well established by 1122, and was probably built before the Norman Conquest at the instigation of Edward the Confesssor (1042-1066), who held the Hundred of Blackburn of which Colne was part.

The Foulridge, or **Tailor's Cross**, was erected in the 13th century as a preaching cross by Peter de Cestria (Rector of Whalley from 1235 to 1294) on the southern edge of the village and served as a field kirk where the people of Foulridge could hold open air services, and where funerals could rest on their way to Colne churchyard for burial.

Cistercian monks had been granted the **Barnside** estate in 1258 (hence the name Monkroyd), and they also had a considerable settlement at Admergill to the NW of Foulridge, where the buildings included a grange and a friary rest house. The Cistercians were great wool producers and they probably used the estates for sheep farming. It seems, however, that the monks did not remain long at Barnside and they subsequently sublet to other tenants. By the time of the Dissolution of the Monasteries the Townley family was in possession.

Foulridge Cross in its original position in Kirk Field. The cross was removed in 1931. The open-air church gave rise to the place names Kirk Bridge and. Little Church Bridge Brook (the former name for Bar Beck)

Detail of doorway at Ball House bearing the initials of John Moore and his wife Ann.

Non-conformity

Dissent with the established church during the 16th and 17th centuries led to a surge of non-conformity in the district which was strenuously opposed.

It was on the summit of Pendle Hill that George Fox had his famous vision in 1652 of '*a great people to be gathered*' which led to the foundation of the Society of Friends or **Quakers**.

An early mention of Quakers in Foulridge occurs in 1662 when **John Moore of Ball House**, a blind preacher, was arrested for refusing to swear an oath and had some goods confiscated for non-payment of church tithes. He was committed to Lancaster Castle where he was imprisoned for more than eleven weeks.

A **Quaker Meeting House** was erected in Foulridge in 1666 in Ivegate (on the site now occupied by Belmont Terrace) and there was a burial ground on the other side of the lane below Pleasant View.

Another celebrated Quaker preacher was **John Barcroft** (1663-1723) who was descended from the Barcrofts of Noyna and visited his cousin, Ambrose Barcroft, then High Constable, in 1690 and on later occasions.

Despite the fact that **Catholics** in the district continued to incur the displeasure of the Church long after the Dissolution of the Monasteries, a number of Foulridge families – notably the Townleys of Barnside, the Holgates and Mancknowls – remained constant in their faith. In 1737 Ann Hartley, John Holgate, William Hyrd, Ellen Windle and William Starkie, all of Foulridge, were excommunicated.

Dissenters' Well

High on Kelbrook Moor, beside the Tom Cross, stands the Dissenters' Well. The Tom Cross was a boundary stone on the old Yorkshire/Lancashire border. The well dates to the time when there was a great deal of animosity towards all non-conformists – Quakers, Catholics, Baptists and Methodists alike – and legislation was passed which made it illegal for their religious gatherings to be held within a 5-mile radius of any Parish Church, leading to gatherings in such bleak and remote places on the moors. It was not until 1812 that various Acts of Parliament against non-conformists were repealed and dissenters were given equality with regard to liberty of worship.

In the 18th century a small but thriving sect of **British Israelites** held gatherings in Breeze House barn. The barn became known as Joanna's Chapel after **Joanna Southcott** (1748-1814), an infamous religious fanatic who had a notion that she was about to give birth to Shiloh, the Messiah of Peace. (In actual fact her expectant appearance was caused by dropsy.) Despite various rather dubious stories about members of the sect, it had more than 14,000 followers and Mr Barcroft of Noyna married his daughter to William Tillotson of Great Horton, who appears to have been a Southcottian and later a follower of John Wroe.

The late 18th century saw the spread of **Methodism** in the district. **Mary Barritt**, born at Hey Fold in 1772, was to become the first lady evangelist in the district, and married the Rev. Zachariah Taft. Mary's father was opposed to Wesleyan Methodism and disapproved of lady preachers. Finally he told her that unless she stopped her preaching she would never enter through his door again. In spite of this Mary left home, but when there was a later reconciliation her father had the doorway at Hey Fold walled up so that his word should not be broken.

Mary's eldest brother, **John Barritt** (b.1756) was one of John Wesley's itinerant preachers for more than fifty years. He also clashed with his father who tempted him not to become a preacher by offering him one of his farms. John accepted, took the farm and married, but within a year his wife died leaving him with an eight day old little girl. John accepted this as 'the voice of God' and became a travelling preacher. He suffered many personal tragedies; both his second and third wives died on circuit. Finally after a ministry of some 55 years he retired back to Owlet Farm and founded the tiny, moorside **Mount Pleasant Chapel** as his personal church. The chapel remained in the family for generations until it became Methodist property in 1880.

Mrs Mary Taft (nee Barritt) from the frontispiece of her Memoirs, a small volume published in 1827 recording her part in the 'new fangled religion of Methodism'

Below left:
The final service at the chapel, 8 June 2008.

Below right:
Mount Pleasant Methodist Chapel at County Brook was founded by the Rev. John Barritt. The chapel was converted from a pair of cottages and opened in 1822.

Foulridge Methodist Chapel erected in 1872, on the site of an earlier chapel dating to 1825, was in the centre of the village. It was demolished in 1983, the victim of dry rot. Towngate Mews were built on the site.

In its heyday the chapel played an important role in the everyday lives of the Whitemoor community, where social events as well as worship took place. On the chapel's anniversary day the services were held out of doors as there was not enough room inside for all those who wanted to attend. The chapel was licensed to conduct weddings, funerals and christenings in 1932. In its latter years congregation numbers dwindled. The final service was held in June 2008.

Foulridge Methodist Chapel

In 1824 a plot of land was purchased in the centre of Foulridge, beside the new turnpike road, to erect a Wesleyan chapel and the building was completed that same year. Alterations were made in 1859 and more land was acquired in 1872 to rebuild. The Chapel had a strong following and enjoyed full congregations every Sunday with regular concerts and operettas. There was also a youth club, football, cricket and tennis clubs connected with the chapel, but gradually after the Second World War the numbers of children in the village began to fall. Services at Foulridge Methodist Chapel came to an end at the beginning of 1983, the building becoming the victim of dry rot and a declining congregation.

Foulridge Church

For centuries followers of the established church travelled to Colne Parish Church, or attended services in the field kirk beside Kirk Bridge.

In 1836 **Christ Church** was built to serve the eastern area of the ancient chapelry. St Mary's at Trawden opened in 1846 but Foulridge remained 'a village without a church' and continued to be served by the clergy of Christ Church with services conducted in the National School on Town Top and, prior to that, at Breeze House.

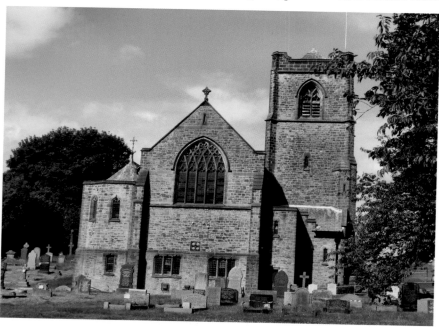

St Michael and All Angels was consecrated in 1905.

The village was split between the parishes of St Bartholomew and Christ Church – Skipton Road being the dividing line between the two ecclesiastical districts. It was not until the beginning of the 20th century that the village got its own church.

Alfred Blackham was the first lay reader appointed at the School in 1898. He was followed by Mr Watson in 1901 and by Rev. David Hall in 1902. On arrival Rev Hall concentrated his energies on the building of the church. By Easter 1903 fundraising had met with such a splendid response that building works commenced. The **Stone Laying Ceremony** took place on Saturday, July 18th, 1903. It was a stirring time. A Procession of both local and Church people from other parishes marched round the village with brass band and banner. Gilt commemorative medals were made to mark the occasion. The stone-laying was performed by Bishop Pearson of Burnley, and addresses were given by the Rev W Clifford and Mr Edward Carr, JP.

The Church was consecrated on 22 May 1905 by Bishop Knox of Manchester and dedicated to **St Michael and All Angels**. The building cost £6,000 and was really quite an achievement when you bear in mind that there were only 400 houses in the village at the time. Designed by R B Preston (who also designed Holy Trinity on Burnley Road in Colne), Pevsner considered the church *"an excellent, quite personal composition to the east, taken in as one approaches the church"*.

The Churchyard was consecrated a few months later, on 9 December 1905, by Bishop Pearson of Burnley.

The Churchyard Cross bears the inscription 'In memory of Mary Ada Carr of the Coppy, Colne 1915'. This was Edward Carr's sister who gave very generously towards the building of St Michael's. Apparently without her help Foulridge Church might have been an iron church built on the site of the old primary school on Town Top.

Foulridge Youth Club was re-formed in 2008 by former village PC Mark Whitehead and a team of volunteers, with financial assistance from Foulridge Parish Council, Lancashire County Council, Pendle Council and donations of equipment from local businesses. The youth club meets every Monday evening in St Michael's Rooms, underneath the church.

The churchyard cross.

Whitsuntide Walk 1950s.

Vicars of Foulridge

The first vicar, David Alston Hall, came to Foulridge as the first Curate in Charge in 1902 and laboured with the masons to build the church. He had the lovely nickname of '*Ping Pong*' which he gained when he first came to the village and was lodging at Accornley because he used to take some children on there to play table tennis. A Church Magazine subsequently recorded that during his incumbency he had officiated at 363 baptisms, 62 marriages, and 200 burials. Peter Wightman drolly commented "*A net gain of 163 with a promise of things to come. I wonder if parsons' promotions are based on piece work?*"

Foulridge has had eleven Vicars:

The Vicarage

The first vicarage was at Edmund's Villa. The site adjoining the churchyard was purchased by subscription in 1910 and the present vicarage completed in 1914.

Three former vicars of Foulridge, from left to right, Keith Palmer, Roy McClure and Derek Raitt.

1. Rev David Alston Hall, MA
Curate in Charge 1902 – 1905
Vicar 1905 – 1917

2. Rev Joseph Gough, MA
1917 – 1937

3. Rev Richard Kirkham
1937 – 1943

4. Rev Victor Marquis
1944 – 1958

Harry Webb, the Headmaster, kept the services going during the period between Rev Marquis' death and the arrival of Canon Williams.

5. Rev Canon Hugh Williams, AKC
1958 – 1965

6. Rev John Brian Selvey, BA
1965 – 1969

7. Rev Derek Raitt
1969 – 1974

8. Rev Keith Palmer
1974 – 1982

9. Rev Roy McClure
1982 – 1988

Rev Richard Allen
Priest in Charge during the Interregnum

10. Rev Wilfred 'Bill' Nuttall
1989 – 1991

11. Rev George Senior
1992 – 1997

Rev John Priestly
Priest in Charge
1997 – 1999

Then in common with many churches throughout the country, smaller congregations and fewer clergy led to the formation of the Colne & Villages Team Ministry covering the five local churches of St Bartholomew's, Holy Trinity, Christh Church, St Mary's Trawden and St Michael & All Angels. In 2008 the Rev. Tony Rindl succeeded the Rev. Mike Hartley as the Team Rector. The Team Priest is Revd Priestly Brook.

Chapter 12

SCHOOLDAYS

The Old School on Town Top

A proposal circulated in 1852 to erect a school in the village drew attention to the fact that '*Each Township within the Chapelry of Colne except poor Foulridge has got its Church, its resident Clergyman, and one National School or more .... Foulridge is now the only Township remaining destitute of religious and educational means*'.

The population was not particularly wealthy, consisting chiefly of handloom weavers, watermen and small farmers, but grants were obtained from government sources and the National Society (Church of England); local landowners also made generous donations. Major Edward Parker of Alkincoats gave land on Town Top known as Further Intake and the building of the National School commenced in 1853. It opened in September 1855.

The school log book for those early years is revealing. Pupils were frequently absent in winter '*gathering sticks*' for fuel, and in summer '*haymaking*'. Many children worked half time in one of the village mills. Lessons consisted mainly of the three 'R's' plus scripture and geography (Europe). The 4th class also received a lesson '*on the pig*'.

A new wing and schoolmaster's house was added in 1884, and in 1896 an Infant School was built for the increase in population that the New Shed had brought to the village.

The Old School on Town Top was built as a National School It opened on 22 September 1855.

Foulridge School class, head teacher Charles Spencer, 1913.

Foulridge School Trip to Blackpool, 1922. A classic photograph by Charles Green showing the Foulridge contingent of children setting off from Town Top to join a convoy of 32 charabancs from Colne and Trawden for the annual outing to the seaside.

The school was a National (Church of England) School and Methodists preferred to send their children to the Sunday School attached to Foulridge Wesleyan Chapel. When education became compulsory many Methodist children walked several miles past the village school to attend non-conformist schools in Colne such as the George Street Wesleyan Day School (opened in 1871) or the Board School at Black Lane Ends which opened in 1900 for 60 children.

Prior to Foulridge Church being built in 1905 services were held in the school, and in 1920 the school officially changed its name and became Foulridge C of E school.

Head Teachers

The earliest schoolmasters were John Woodward and John Veevers, followed at the end of the19th century by **Arthur Whitworth**, who combined his post at the school with that of Clerk to Foulridge Parish Council. In 1899 he was summoned for persistent cruelty to his wife. He was apparently in the habit of coming home mad drunk at night, pulling his wife about, cursing her and the children and threatening their lives, and had so completely terrified them that they had to flee to seek protection in neighbours' houses. He had taken upstairs the paraffin lamp, swung it over the bed in which his wife and daughters were lying, and threatened to burn the house down. The Parish Council Minutes refer obliquely to the incident and hint of further scandal when he suddenly vanished from the scene as Clerk. The Minutes cryptically state that *the [new] Clerk demand the Books from Mr Whitworth*, and at a later meeting it was *moved that the last Clerk, Mr Whitworth, be prosecuted*.

School Group c.1921 assembling in playground prior to setting off on annual school outing organised by the Colne Children's Treat Committee. The younger children wore labels in the event of becoming separated from their classmates.

Later pupils at the school were more fortunate in their schoolmasters. Although ruling with a firm hand Charles Spencer, Ellis Fell and Ernest Holden are recalled with great respect and all made tremendous personal contributions to village life.
Charles Spencer (1899-1930) was also Organist and Choirmaster at Foulridge Church for more than 40 years and, following his retirement as head teacher, he ran the village Post Office with his wife who was the village postmistress.

Ellis Fell (1930-53) headed the school throughout the Second World War when evacuee children from Bradford and Manchester were merged into the school. He was a driving force behind one of the village's most famous institutions – the Five F's (the Foulridge Fight for Freedom Fund) as well as Clerk to the Parish Council for many years.

Senior Class, 1936. Ellis Fell was the Head Master.

Foulridge Senior School 1936

Miss Mcleans Class

Back Row	Centre Row	Front Row
1 Danny Foster	10 Olive Brown	20 Geoffrey Green
2 Colin Hartley	11 Louie Greenwood	21 Ronald Thackary
3 Norman Fishwick	12 Sheila Walsh	22 Alfred Smith
4 Jim Hartley	13 Thora Lumley	23 Gordon Ellis
5 Alan Barke	14 Irene Cox	24 Alwyn Tomlinson
6 Sidney Cox	15 Dorothy Charnock	
7 Harold Jobling	16 Eleanor Powell	
8 Donald Wilkinson	17 Isobel Wilkinson	
9 Arnold Smith	18 Joyce Bleasdale	
	19 Nora Pratt	

Foulridge senior school group 1936.

Foulridge school group 1967. Teacher, Helen Henshaw.

Foulridge school 1976–77. Teacher, Marshal Brown.

The school originally catered for infants, juniors and seniors up to the age of 14. In 1945 the school became a primary school and older children transferred to Colne schools from the age of 11. Ellis Fell retired in December 1953 after 23 years.

Harry Webb was head from 1954 to 1958, followed by **Ernest Holden** who came to the school in 1959 and was headmaster for almost 24 years. He was secretary of the Village Hall Committee, the Parochial Church Council and the Working Men's Club and during his time saw many changes at the school including the number of children and staff double.

Foulridge school 1977, Jubilee Year.

The 'New' School

Overcrowding had been a problem for some time. The battle for a new school, which had begun in 1920, continued for more than fifty years, and the major landmark in the life of the school came when it moved from the old building to its present site on 8th August 1978. It brought to a close an era spanning 122 years of learning in the village. The old school which had served past generations had done its job.

The move was not however without complications. When eventually the new school was ready to open, Lancashire County Council stated that there was a regulation which prohibited the old site being completely abandoned until it was officially sold. Astonishingly therefore for two months the fourth year juniors had to remain at the old building for their lessons while the rest of the children started at the new school. Every morning and afternoon come rain or shine, Marshal Brown and his class tramped the half mile between the two buildings.

The new school had been built in the late 1950s as the Holy Rosary Convent, and subsequently housed a training school for postulants. Following refurbishment, the new village school officially opened in 1978. Shortly afterwards the name changed to **St Michael & All Angels C of E Primary School**.

The new school had been built in the late 1950s as the Holy Rosary Convent, and subsequently housed a training school for postulants. Following refurbishment, the 'New' school officially opened in 1978.

Foulridge school staff c.1982. Head Kathleen Allen

The school has only had ten head teachers in its 155 year history. When **Kathleen Allen** became the new Head in September 1982, she had the distinction of being the first ever female to be in charge of the whole school. Mrs Allen retired in 1994, and in the same year she became Colne's first woman priest. She was succeeded by **Anne Wells**, and ten years later by the current Head Teacher **Hilary Woods**.

St Michael & All Angels remains a popular and happy school with high educational standards and, unlike many village schools that have closed in recent years, its future is secure. It remains as a tribute to the hard work and dedication of its staff.

Chapter 13

PUBS PAST AND PRESENT

Making the Bowling Green.

In the early 1900s social life in the village thrived and there was a variety of village institutions and organizations including the Social Working Men's Club, a Weavers' Institute (a non-drinking establishment for young men) held in the Tin Tab, Conservative and Liberal Clubs, an Ambulance Division, a Church Institute founded by the Rev Hall on Town Top, a Wesleyan Sunday School and Methodist Institute, which closed in1927 when the billiard table was sold for £11.

Foulridge Working Men's Club started life as the Towngate Club in 1908 when it was converted from a co-op storage area. A group of local men built the bowling green at the back of the club by hand, which took them several months, working every evening and weekends for no pay. This photograph captures them carrying out the work.

One of the biggest laughs of 1990 came when phantom moles struck at the bowling green. Three 'hills' made by the nocturnal small creatures were found and left club officials flabbergasted. But not for long, for they realized it was April Fools Day! Up until 1993 the club was men only and women could only enter on Christmas draw night. Now known as Foulridge Social Club, the club is now open to both sexes.

Beer Houses

Below left: Former beerhouse at Causeway Cottage with datestone reading 1692.

Below right: The Grinning Rat.

As well as inns the village had a number of beer houses – at Standing Stone Gate, on Town Top, Causeway and at the end of Cromwell Street. Causeway Cottage, which dates to 1692, became an alehouse frequented by the canal navvies and

The Dog and Gun, at the Warehouse Lane end of Cromwell Street bearing the sign of Samuel Crabtree who ran the beer house in the late 1800s. The 1851 Census lists Hargreaves Crook at the beer house in 'Crummel Square'. The building had ceased to be a beer house by the time Walton Barritt came to live there during the First World War.

later by boatmen. It was also a 'doss house' providing cheap lodging.

The coming of the canal saw other beerhouses open including the gloriously named Grinning Rat and Slip Inn at either end of the Foulridge tunnel. **The Slip Inn**, sited on the canal bank near Foulridge Wharf , remained in use throughout the 19th century, whilst the Grinning Rat at Wanless reverted to its original use as a farmhouse. **The Grinning Rat** quenched the thirst of 500 navvies who came to repair the tunnel in 1824 when 'the floor began to rise'. The work took seven months and much had to be re-excavated and strengthened. It took the ale of three loads of malt weekly to keep the men going and it seems that not all of this was honestly bought and paid for. There is an indisputable tradition that some of the vats of whisky which the barges carried were tapped at this place, and the spirit exchanged for the landlord's more workmanlike brew. The whisky later found itself sold at cut price in the many taverns of nearby Colne.

The Rose & Crown featured in the 1968 BBC TV's serialization of Anne Bronte's classic 'The Tenant of Wildfell Hall', and for a short time Noyna Bottom Farm became the fictional 'The Rose and Crown'.

The original Hole in the Wall demolished at the turn of the 19th century. The name can just be made out on the side of the building. The W.M.C building was then the village Co-Op and the chimneys behind the pub were part of Foulridge washhouse and bake house.

The Hole in the Wall, November 2005, boasting not only a new sign on the side of the building dedicated to 'Buttercup', but also the official Post Office sign.

Village Inns

Inns and public houses were an essential part of village life. They provided refreshment and accommodation for both man and beast. All three village pubs were in existence by the 1820s.

The original **Hole in the Wall** on Towngate was probably the oldest, said to date to the 1600s. The inn gained its name from the nearby 'Mile' tunnel for that is how it appears from its northern end. The original pub, which clearly had an earlier name before the tunnel was constructed, was knocked down to make way for the pub built in 1899. The stables and outbuildings, used by, among others, one Charlie '*Bloodtub*' Irving, a local fruiterer, were demolished more recently for a car park.

John and Ruth Richmond held the licence from 1891 to about 1925, during the period when the old pub was rebuilt. The longest serving landlords were **Jack and Nora Shaw** who retired in 1984 after 26 years. Lorenzo, Jack's pet parrot, caused quite a flutter at the local, particularly when he burst into a rendition of 'God Save the Queen'. During 2005 landlords Stephen and Christine Letch, provided Post Office facilities in the pub, but the experiment was short-lived and the Post Office relocated at the end of the year.

The last tenants departed in 2007 and the pub stood empty. It was demolished in January 2010 and current proposals are for a mix of three-storey apartments and houses on the site.

New Inn.

The **'New' Inn** is older than the name suggests and was probably so-named as being a *new* building on the site of an earlier inn. A 'To Let' poster exists which shows it was obviously well established in 1816 when the tenant was a John Spencer, an ancestor of the late Wilfred Spencer, who spent a spell in the House of Correction for refusing to maintain his illegitimate twins by a young servant girl at Cragg. He was already married to Barbara Elliott, whom he left in charge of the New Inn, and she fell in with some counterfeit coin makers from Manchester. The inn gained a reputation for being a **forgers' den** when she began to issue counterfeit coins in with the change, as a result of which the couple were apparently transported.

From the 1880s until the early 1900s Hartley Barritt, an ancestor of the present Barritts of Hey Farm, kept the New Inn and had boats on the canal transporting coal and stone. Popular landlords in recent years include Jack Harrison, and John and Marie Forsyth. The inn underwent a major make-over in 2007 but temporarily closed in May 2008 following the ill health of the licensee Barry Shepherd, who had been the landlord for more than ten years.

The New Inn features in 'Haunted Inns of England' as being one of the most haunted pubs in Lancashire and there are innumerable tales of restless spirits who refuse to be laid to rest.

Purportedly dating to the late 1600s, the **Hare and Hounds** was certainly in existence by 1824, when it was used by coaches using the new *Colne & Broughton Turnpike road*. The name suggests the pub was patronized by the gentlemen of the district before they went hare coursing, a very popular sport in the 18th and 19th centuries.

John Mancknowls of the Cragg left a Memoranda Book which contains a number of references to the Hare and Hounds; the most interesting being in 1863 when it changed hands. He recorded how the then landlord, John Waterhouse,

New Inn 'To be Let' poster, 1816

The Hare and Hounds.

was unable to pay all his creditors and attempted to remove brewing utensils and other items from the pub before the bailiffs made distraint. The goods were hidden at the Hole in the Wall but were seized at the station en route to Bradford.

Subsequent landlords include **Abner Brunskill Barritt** in the early 1900s, who farmed Breeze House while his wife ran the inn, and **Irene Whittam**, Pendle's longest serving landlady, who was behind the bar from 1959 to 1992.

Since being branded 'the Grottiest pub in Britain' the pub has undergone a series of refurbishments which have transformed the building. The old smithy and stables at the rear, once occupied by horses, now provide kitchen and guest facilities. The pub

The village smithy at the rear of the Hare & Hounds c.1900. Photo by Charles Green.

The Hargreaves Arms, July 1981. The bunting was for the Royal Wedding celebrations of Prince Charles and Lady Diana Spencer.

has been awarded entry into Camra's Good Beer Guide and was recently nominated for a good food award for its in-house restaurant.

All Foulridge pubs originally had their own brewhouses and made their own beer on the premises. By 1874 however the village had its own brewery, the **Croft Well Brewery** 'Ale & Porter Brewers' established in premises which had earlier been the Croft Weaving mill. In 1879 the brewery was owned by Bannister Jackson and managed by Edward Bird who lived at Close House. The brewery was later bought by Alexander Bell, brewer of Barrowford, who demolished it in 1888 for the erection of Belmont Terrace.

Early trade directories list the **Hargreaves Arms** under Foulridge when the Monkroyd area was still part of the Foulridge Detached. The inn was part of the Barnside estate which was owned by the Every-Claytons (hence its earlier name the *Clayton Arms*). It was bought in 1840 by the Hargreaves family who promptly changed its name. The next record of sale came in 1911 when a Colne farmer, Edward Pickles, bought the inn with '*bar, tap room, billiards room, four bedrooms, piggeries and accommodation for six horses and twenty four cattle.*' He sold it to John Smith's Tadcaster Brewery in 1935. The Hargreaves Arms was almost destroyed by a devastating fire in 2004, and did not reopen as a public house.

Chapter 14

SPORT AND RECREATION

Eric and Ruth Stanworth with their son Mark when the stables won a British Horse Society approval in the early 1990s.

The very name of the village suggests that from early times Foulridge was a place where horses were bred. Indeed until the First World War trotting horses were trained near Noyna End and races were regularly held through the village. These were however officially frowned upon as being dangerous; in 1879 Joss Windle and John Sutcliffe were summoned and charged for each 'racing a horse furiously on Foulridge highway'.

Horses are still a common sight locally. The livery, established by the Stanworths at Whitemoor Bottom Farm in 1977, developed into **Whitemoor Riding School** which opened in 1991 offering instruction in riding and jumping. Ruth Stanworth specialises in producing show horses from hacks and riding horses to hunter ponies, and preparing riders for shows and competitions including the national championships. She was placed 4th at the Horse of the Year Show in 2005 with her husband's coloured traditional cob.

In recent years Carole England has been responsible for getting three **bridleways** in Foulridge officially designated. Bridleway 42 starts at Skipton Road, crosses Skipton Old Road and continues up over Hallam Moor to join the Noyna Bottom Road, and continues to Laneshawbridge. Bridleways 43 & 44 commence at Skipton Old Road at Greenhead cottage and run parallel to Teddy Carr Drive behind Ambwell Farm out onto Cob Lane, and past Kelbrook Shooting Lodge eventually meeting the road by the Black Lane Ends pub.

Ancient sports included **archery**, which took place on the village butts to the south of Town Gate, and **bull-baiting** which was practised at Breeze House. **Cockfighting** was another popular 'sport' and during the 18th century the lanes of Foulridge were filled with the carriages of gentry who had ridden over to see 'a main' fought between two game birds.

Hare coursing was particularly popular in the village, the sport giving its name to the village inn. In the 1800s John Mancknowls of Cragg (who owned the Hare & Hounds) kept a pack of harriers and it is more than likely that the hounds congregated outside the inn prior to the hunt.

From prehistoric times the moors surrounding Foulridge provided hunters with ample game and sport. There are still two **grouse moors** within the boundary of the village – White Moor, and what used to be known as Teddy Carr's Moor, at the end of the old coach road above Noyna. The Shooting Box itself was purpose built in 1908 for shooting entertainment days by Edward Carr of Langroyd. A century later the Victorian tradition continues and **Kelbrook Shooting Lodge** is now one of the North West's foremost venues for clay pigeon shooting. This family business is run by Michael Meggison, a member of the British Olympic

Kelbrook Shooting Lodge

Shooting team in 1980 and 1984 and his son, Aaron, who has had great success in the British team and Commonwealth championships since the age of 13.

As well as hunting and shooting, **fishing** was a popular pastime, even before the building of the reservoirs. Foulridge Brook, later known as King's Beck, flowed into Marsden Close in the valley bottom near Hobstones, and Elizabeth Shackleton recorded that her husband frequently fished there in the second half of the 18th century. The Boat House at Slipper Hill was used as a shooting and fishing lodge by the Directors of the Canal Company – hence the unusual weather vane above the building.

Both the fishing and boating rights for Burwains Reservoir were owned by the Clayton family of Carr Hall from 1799 to 1886, and rules included stipulations that no one was allowed to fish before 7.00 a.m. and only one rod was to be used by each angler. Fishing was obviously very much a gentleman's sport as to fish on Burwains Reservoir cost 3s 6d per day. Day tickets had to be bought from the Red Lion Hotel in Colne. In 1886 the boating and fishing rights passed to Edward Carr, who bequeathed them to his gamekeeper, Jim Haigh, nicknamed Kimmick. The 'res' remains a popular venue for coarse fishing matches. Teddy Carr also had fishing rights to the Upper and Brown Hill reservoirs, and it was he who granted Colne anglers a lease which still exists.

Burwains Reservoir has been the centre for numerous sports since its creation. In winter villagers would skate, whilst in summer they swam or hired a boat for a pleasant Sunday afternoon trip. During the 1920s and 30s Jim Haigh had a hut on the Colne side of Kirk Bridge, beside the present existing gate, from which he hired rowing boats. Part of the hut was allotted to Mrs Betsy Hargreaves who ran a small tea-shop supplying sweets, crisps and jugs of tea for those who simply wanted to walk around the reservoir.

A small sailing club existed pre 1939 at the Kirk Bridge end of the 'lake'. The originator was a Mr Summerscales of Keighley who brought his Abersoch One

Right: Lake Burwain.

design from North Wales on a lorry. **Burwain Sailing Club** was reformed in 1952 at the Hobstones end of the reservoir, the first clubhouse being a marquee tent. The present clubhouse was rebuilt in 1984. During the early days of the club they sailed only two classes of dinghies – the 12' Gunter rigged 'Burnham' and the 12' Bermuda rigged 'Firefly'. The club now has a wide variety of fleets which compete regularly including the Mirror, Solo, GP14, Laser, Topper, Mixed handicap and the occasional windsurfer! It prides itself as being a friendly club and encourages young people to take to the water. Their waterborne Santa is always a hit at the children's Christmas party.

Ted Fort joined Burwain Sailing Club at the age of 18 and learnt his sailing skills there. His love of sailing which began in Foulridge led him to become an Olympic class sailor. In 1973 he was selected to help crew the Soling type yacht 'Surprise' in the European Sailing Championships, and in 1977 he qualified for the Olympic team. He presently competes in Dragons and Etchells. In 2009 he was the proud recipient of the Docker Cup, a prestigious award from the Royal

Club members on the pontoon at Burwain Sailing Club, 1961/2. From left to right: Robin Delves, Sheila Noble, ? Hill, Harold Evan Jones, Betty Smith, Roger Harris, Tony Bancroft, Christine Delves, John Reed, Max Uttley, Laurie Lord, Jim Akrill, Jack Cockcroft, Jack Binns, Ted Fort unknown, unknown, Harry ?, unknown.

Thames Yacht Club in recognition of his contribution to sailing over the years.

A controversial proposal by British Waterways in 1992 for making money from speed boats and jet skiing on the tranquil reservoir met fierce opposition from all quarters. Long-standing fishing agreements were terminated and for the first time in more than 30 years anglers were thrown off the reservoir as a first stage in the plans. Happily the scheme was subsequently withdrawn.

Canal cruises are not new. The canal was popular for Sunday School trips, and Canal Company shareholders were regularly entertained aboard the steam launch 'Waterwitch'. **Foulridge Leisure Cruises** continues the long tradition.

Pendle Paddlers were formed in 1997 by a group of canoe and kayakers who used to meet in the Burnley Canoe Centre. During the summer months they hold weekly club nights on the Leeds and Liverpool Canal at Foulridge Wharf where they have a club boathouse. With over 100 members they cater for a mix of people from age 8 onwards with different kayaking and canoeing skills

Joan Wilkinson

Joan Wilkinson progressed from learning the basics of cricket in the 1930s on the recreation ground (then sited in the field in front of her house on Reedymoor Terrace) to gaining an international reputation as a leading member of the England women's team and meeting cricket legends such as Sir Donald Bradman. At the outbreak of the Second World War Joan volunteered to join the Women's Auxiliary Air Force but was turned down because of her height- she stood a mere 4ft 11 1/2 in. Then they heard of her sporting prowess and she was called up in 1941. Her military duties were to instruct her WAAFs in cricket, hockey and PT, and her cricketing career blossomed.

After the war Joan remained in the WAAF (later the WRAF), which released her whenever she was called upon to play for England. She was selected for the 1948/9 tour of Australia and New Zealand. The journey out to Australia was by sea, via the Suez Canal and the return was via the Panama Canal, thus circumnavigating the globe. She was vice-captain of England in the 1950s. Her final appearance for her country was the 1957/8 New Zealand tour.

First Test Adelaide Oval, Australia 1949. Some of WCA Touring team meet Sir Donald Bradman, (Joan Wilkinson extreme left)

Before the **bowling green** was built on Town Gate, Noyna quarries provided a good hideaway for another form of bowling – bowling on the highway or 'bairlin', a sport banned by various Acts of Parliament. But law or no law the game went on until about the 1920s and men gathered well out of the reach of the arm of the law. There was gambling on a large scale. Enthusiasm ran high and often wagers ran as high as £50 a side – an enormous sum in those days. The gambling activities gave rise to the local nickname **Monte Carlo**.

Virtually from the time of its inception the Parish Council was concerned with the provision of a **recreation ground** for the village and, over the years was involved in protracted negotiations to secure a suitable site. At the beginning of the 1900s a field at Reedymoor was used for football, cricket and tennis, and in 1912 land adjacent to the National school was purchased from the Parkers. It was felt, however, that there should be a playing field as well as a 'rec'. In 1946 the Parish Council was offered the surplus from the Five F's towards the cost of purchasing a playing field. Efforts were made to purchase Bradley Butts meadow and land attached to both Reedymoor and Waller Hill farms. It was finally resolved to purchase the piece of land on the east side of the Recreation Ground owned by Mr W Blackburn.

Foulridge Cricket Club was formed in 1956 and is part of the Craven & District League. The Michael Hook Memorial Trophy is awarded for the person who has done most for the club throughout the year. 1983 was a memorable year for the Club when both the First and Second teams were cup winners; the 1st team won the Wynn Cup and the 2nd team won the Cowling cup. Sadly the year also witnessed the old cricket pavilion destroyed by fire. It was rebuilt in 1986 by Pendle Re-employment project. In 2000 Foulridge had 3 Cricket Club Teams – Foulridge 1st Team, Foulridge Seconds, and Cricket Youth Team.

The Bowling Green behind Foulridge Social Club on Towngate

Foulridge Cricket Club 1st & 2nd Teams Cup Winners 1983

Foulridge Football Club, first team, Reedymoor Lane early 1900s.

The old **Foulridge Football Club** was known as 'the Wasps' because of the yellow and black striped shirts. Originally they played at Reedymoor, then at Broach Flatt Farm (at the back of the new school), and the last season was on Alan Wilson's field at the bottom of Cocker Hill.

In 1995 **Foulridge Minors** were founded and coached by former Colne Dynamos midfielder John Garnett. In 2000 the team boasted one of the best junior sides in the local Burnley Warburton's Youth League and players were signed to Blackburn Rovers and Leicester City.

Bobbins and Reelers, 1994 For centuries both Maypole and Morris Dancing took place on Towngate. Happily this tradition continues with the Bobbins and Reelers Morris Dancers founded by Graham and Margaret Cannon

Official Launch of the Beating the Bounds Leaflet by Cllr Allan Buck, Mayor of Pendle, 2008

There was also a Girls Football team and a Boys team. At the time of writing all the football teams have disbanded.

The Parish Council has a long tradition of protecting **public footpaths** which has often been an emotive issue. In 1910-14 disputes arose when attempts were made to close various footpaths around Old Ebby's, Foulridge Reservoir, Reef Edge and Noyna. Each Saturday some 50 or so villagers would walk along the footpaths pulling down the barricades and obstructions. The landowners who blocked the footpaths were powerful and influential, and it took men of courage who were prepared if necessary to go to prison to preserve their rights. Such men included Henry Banks, William Hook and Frank Eastwood, whose relatives withdrew what little money they had in the bank and even sold their furniture for fear of it being seized following the case which reached the High Court at Liverpool. In the event a settlement was reached whereby the Canal Company dedicated the footpaths around the reservoirs forever,

Walking remains popular today. The original 45 mile Pendle Way route followed the borough boundary and so gave Foulridge a wide berth, but in 1989 one of the circular routes dropped into Foulridge around the reservoir and along the canal to Barrowford. In 2008 the ancient tradition of **Beating the Bounds** was revived and a walking leaflet, jointly sponsored by Pendle Borough Council and the Parish Council, was officially launched by the Mayor of Pendle.

Chapter 15

A VILLAGE IN WARTIME

When war was declared on 4 August 1914 local men responded readily. By November 1914 **Alderman Henry Hewitt-Dean**, who had recently moved to the newly built Kirk Rise, offered his former home in Colne (now the offices of the Britannia Building Society) to the Voluntary Aid Detachment to become the **Colne Auxiliary Military Hospital**. The hospital was obviously well run by **Dr Dickey**, resident surgeon at Colne Cottage Hospital on Barrowford Road, and nursing staff assisted by VADs; out of 853 patients only two deaths occurred and those were caused by influenza!

The Colne & Nelson Times published weekly lists of names of the men who joined His Majesty's Forces. Following the sinking of the *Lusitania* in 1915 the list was exceptionally long.

Near the canal towpath '*The Bottoms*' between Foulridge and Salterforth became the site of a **munitions depot** (cordite dump) with storage huts and a single track railway line which ran to Kelbrook junction, and Foulridge Methodist Chapel gained the curious distinction of being one of the few buildings insured against zeppelin raids.

Tom Draper was allowed to leave school prematurely to help his father with the Foulridge Tunnel Tug in the vital task of ferrying through war supplies, and later said his favourite relief jobs were grooming and feeding the tow horses stabled at the bottom of Warehouse Lane.

The '**Tipperary Club**' was formed to provide local men serving overseas with 'comforts' such as socks, balaclavas and tobacco and give those at home an opportunity to feel they were '*doing their bit*'.

By the time conscription came into force in January 1916 many Foulridge men had already enlisted in the East Lancashire, Lancashire Fusiliers and other regiments. Although a number served in the R.N Sick Berth Reserve, none were on the ill-fated Hospital Ship '*Rohilla*' which ran aground in 1914 and in which twelve Barnoldswick men perished.

Local women typified the national picture – they played an important role at home, working as drivers, on the land and in the cotton mills, doing voluntary work in the military hospital, setting up food centres and organizing fund-raising events for the troops.

By the end of the Great War forty Foulridge men had lost their lives, more than half in the trenches of the Somme and on battlefields on the Western Front. In a village with a population of less than 1500 virtually every family would have been touched by the loss.

Official Peace Celebrations were held in 1919, but life had changed.

On Saturday 25th September 1926 crowds of people attended the **Official Unveiling and Dedication of the War Memorial**. The prime mover in having a public memorial erected in the village was Mr W A Pilgrim, whose only child, Stephen Argent Pilgrim, was killed in 1918, aged only 19.

Lest we forget

The Foulridge War Memorial at the top of Lowther Lane is simply inscribed 'To the memory of our men 1914-18, 1939-45' together with the names of those who died for their country.

World War I

Tom Elsworth Armistead
Clarence Baldwin
William Banks
Paul Bannister
Frank Barritt
John Pickles Barritt
John Robert Barritt
John Blackburn
Frank Bracewell
Thomas Marsden Crewe
John Willie Driver
Fred Emmott
Thomas Foster
Samuel Gothorp
Thomas Albert Grindrod
Walter Hargreaves
Enoch Hartley
James Hartley
Jim Johnson
Albert Kimberley

Fred Kimberley
Fred Kneller
Walter Leech
John Lewis
Chester Wray Lonsdale
Walter William Lund
Harry Pickover
Thomas Edward Pickup
Stephen Argent Ffennell Pilgrim
James Leonard Roberts
Ralph Roberts
George Henry Rodgers
Rennie Shuttleworth
Albert Slinger
Samuel Smith
Myers Thompson
Harold Veevers
Albert Walker
Thomas Wildman

World War II

John Banks
Clifford Birch
Herbert Fothergill
James Ernest Fothergill
John Winston Hargreaves
Francis John Slinger
Ernest Calvert Wildman

They shall not grow old as we that are left grow old.

Age shall not weary them, nor the years condemn.

At the going down of the sun and in the morning

we will remember them.

The Foulridge Cenotaph.

Air Raid Precautions (ARP) group outside Breeze House The Air Raid Wardens checked on the blackout and were generally the men on the spot to inform and aid the police, fire and other rescue services.

World War II

In 1936 the German zeppelin **Hindenburg** passed slowly over the district and villagers were astounded to witness the giant airship, ostensibly en route from America to a cemetery in Keighley to drop flowers for WWI prisoners of war who had died in an influenza epidemic. In later years it was suspected that the 'plane was on a spy mission and the more likely purpose for the detour had been to take aerial photographs of northern cities in preparation for war.

An **Air Raids Precautions** (ARP) Committee was formed locally in 1938 and, when war became a reality, an ARP Centre was set up in the Guild Room above the old Co-op at the bottom of Ivegate on Skipton Road and, to comply with blackout restrictions, the lamplighter was instructed to keep street lighting to a minimum.

Bradford was a prime target for bombing raids because of its industrial importance to the war effort and hundreds were evacuated to rural district areas. The first **evacuee children** arrived in Foulridge within days of war being declared. Boys from the Priestman Central School in Bradford arrived at the Ambulance Hall (now the Village Hall) to be welcomed by Mrs Margaret Croasdale, the Billeting Officer, and introduced to their host families. The girls went to Blacko. Great efforts were made locally to make the children welcome - a Joint Sports Day held a fortnight later included a fell race to Blacko Tower, high jump, sack races, three-legged, skipping and obstacle races.

The number on the school roll doubled and it was a credit to Ellis Fell, the Head Master, that the merger into the existing school went so smoothly. On 25th November 1939 the headline in the local paper was '*Evacuation vindicated. Bradford children happy at Foulridge*'. The Teacher in charge of the Bradford evacuee boys stated that '*if the impression has grown in some districts that the evacuation scheme has failed, such a view cannot be taken of it in the case of Foulridge where experiments in education under conditions never before experienced have proved outstandingly successful.*

Lancashire County Special Constabulary, Colne Section 1940. The Lancashire Constabulary were responsible for action in the event of Air Raid damage, unexploded bombs and the landing of enemy troops

Last Saturday a party of evacuees styling themselves the "Priestman Follies" gave an entertainment at Colne which thoroughly delighted an audience of over 600 children. The children prepared all the scenery, costumes, lyrics and music, and the whole programme reached a high standard of excellence'.

By 1940 food rationing had begun, gas masks issued, the **Home Guard** were meeting at the Tin Tabernacle on Causeway, and Lonsdale's Peel Mill was taken over and used as a food storage depot. **Air Raid Shelters** appeared near the Hare & Hounds and on Town Gate, whilst tree guards disappeared from Town Gate to be handed over to agents collecting scrap iron for the Ministry of Supply.

An **Auxiliary Fire Service** was formed to support the Colne Fire Brigade. AFS Fireman Edgar Banks, supported by 'Old' Birch, Rennie Wrigglesworth and Gordon Moorhouse as 'Firewatchers' viewed the searchlights and Manchester Blitz from the Size Room on the top floor of Robert's Mill. Their 'rehearsals' on Warehouse Lane apparently provided some amusement for local folk as the hose was full of holes!

People were encouraged to 'Dig for Victory' and grow their own food, but renting a 'pen' was not without its problems. As well as coping with backache and pilfering, allotment holders had to deal with foraging fowl in search of a free feed. An application to keep a pig on the allotments was granted by the Parish Council *'the tenant to be notified that it was a war measure only'*.

Initially there were few air raids on the cities and this encouraged many families to bring their children back home; the Priestman boys left by July 1940. When bombing started in earnest however, a second evacuation took place. **Alkincoats Hall** became an evacuee hostel, mainly for those from Manchester who had been bombed out, and in January 1941 an influx of 69 boys and girls from Ducie Street School in Manchester arrived on Town Top by double-decker bus. Imagine the delight of the two evacuee girls billeted with Mr and Mrs Harry Bannister at Brantwood, one of the grandest houses in the district!

The nearest bombs were a stick of nine, jettisoned on Pinhaw Moor and one behind Red Scar Works in Colne. In July 1941 the Foulridge Guides were recruited to guard a 'Mile of Pennies' which the 'Voluntary' (WVS) was trying to raise for the Mobile Canteen based at Colne Railway Station. In May 1942 the Guide Logbook recorded *'much interest was aroused in the village by the civil defences who took part in a **Mock Invasion**'*. The Girl Guides, Sea Scouts, Boy Scouts, WVS, ARP, AFS and Colne First Aid Party and two platoons of Home Guard all took part. One platoon attacked as Paratroops, while the other defended. The Guides took part as casualties but as night drew in some had failed to be rescued and went home. The official report was that *'on the whole the exercise was carried out satisfactorily and the various services cooperated very well in carrying out their different duties'*.

Allen Exley, the area organizer for the National Savings movement, organized numerous campaigns locally. Savings Certificates and Bonds were available from Martins Bank. During national **Warships Week** in 1942 the response was magnificent – Britain and Freedom were worth saving for – the people of Colne, Trawden and Foulridge saved a remarkable £327,000 and, as a result, the area was allowed to 'adopt' a new minesweeper, **HMS Colne**. Plaques to this effect were

HMS Colne plaque. The plaque is inscribed 'Presented by the Lords Commissioners of the Admiralty to the Parish of Foulridge to commemorate the adoption of HMS Colne during Warships Week 1942'.

St John Ambulance

The St John Ambulance, Foulridge Corps was formed in 1896 and soon became one of the village's most valued institutions. In its earliest years it was responsible for innumerable fund raising activities in both the old National and Wesleyan schools to raise funds for an Assembly Hall.

There was tremendous support and due to the interest shown by several ladies, classes in First Aid and Home Nursing were held. These proved as popular as the men's classes, and soon a good number of ladies obtained their certificates.

The Ambulance Movement played a valuable role in times of national emergency. During the Boer War seven members of the Foulridge Corps went to South Africa to nurse the sick and wounded, and in the First World War local members volunteered as members of the Sick Berth Reserve and served aboard hospital ships bringing wounded back from France. Others joined the Voluntary Aid Detachment. When Henry Hewitt-Dean of Kirk Rise placed his former Colne residence at the disposal of the VAD, they equipped it as an auxiliary military hospital

placed on board the vessel, and commemorative plaques were sent to Colne and Trawden. Foulridge folk were aggrieved, and understandably so, the village had raised more per head than either Colne or Trawden but had no record of their achievement. The Clerk to the Parish Council wrote to the Admiralty - and the village duly received its own plaque.

Few village institutions are remembered with such pride by local folk or evoke memories of the community spirit during the war more than the **5 F's – the Foulridge Fight for Freedom Fund** set up for the purpose of sending parcels to Foulridge men serving overseas, both in the forces and merchant navy, replacing

Five F's Auctioning a calf on Town Gate

Five F's Poster

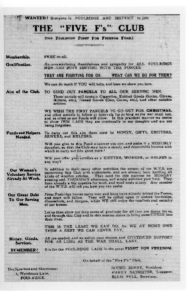

the Tipperary Club of the First World War. The driving forces behind the Fund were Margaret Croasdale, Ellis Fell, Harry Bannister, Sidney Spencer and Jackie Hook; and the entire village soon became involved in this local war effort. Mrs Croasdale organized knitting circles and home knitters to make scarves, socks, pullovers, vests etc; and social functions – whist and beetle drives, dances, raffles, and jumble sales - were arranged to provide other comforts such as tobacco. Auction sales were held in the Ambulance Hall (now the Village Hall) of furniture and 'Black Market' goods such as meat, sugar, eggs and butter - anything that would raise money. Local farmers even auctioned livestock and the authorities appear to have turned a blind eye for such a good cause.

No. 1 Warehouse Lane, the centre for many village activities including the Clinic, Red Cross, Women's Voluntary Service (WVS), and talks on 'Make Do and Mend' and 'Thrift', was also used as the headquarters, store and despatch centre for the 5 F's. **Langroyd Hall** became an emergency Maternity Home for women evacuated from Bradford.

One of the best secrets of the war locally was of three Navy boats which sailed through the Mile Tunnel. Apparently old Mr Draper received a call advising that landing craft would be travelling along the canal to the east coast passing through the tunnel. He offered the services of the Foulridge Tug but was told the vessels had diesel engines, and his warning that the tunnel was poorly ventilated with only three air shafts was dismissed. When the boats emerged at the Foulridge end of the tunnel the crews were overcome by the diesel fumes and were laid out on the canal bank to recover.

The school closed for Victory in Europe (VE Day) on 8 May 1945. By August the Japanese had surrendered. The war was finally over and the country celebrated.

Wilkinson family photo c.1942 l-r David Wilkinson, Hazel, Lance, Joan and mother Maggie (nee Jolly). Lance was on embarkation leave and Joan on leave from the WAAF so, like many families at the time, they had a formal family portrait taken at a local photographic studio as a memento. Hazel wanted to be in uniform so wore her guide uniform.

Thankfully the loss of village life was much less than during the Great War, but seven further names were to be added to the War Memorial.

So successful was the 5 F's effort that after the War a surplus had accumulated and this was offered to the Parish Council towards the purchase of a cricket and football field. After prolonged attempts to acquire suitable land for a recreation ground, the present site on the Noyna road was eventually acquired.

A bus shelter was erected on Reedymoor Lane to the memory of Sir Winston Churchill '*for his indomitable courage in leading the nation to victory in the Great War 1939-1945*'.

Chapter 16

FOULRIDGE PARISH COUNCIL

Walton Barritt.

Foundation stone on Village Hall. The Stone Laying ceremony took place on 22 January 1898 and each of the stone layers – Dr Dickey, Mrs Eleanor Anderton of Burwains, and Edward Carr of Langroyd – were presented with a trowel to mark the occasion. Their initials may be seen on the foundation stones of the building. Beneath one of the stones is a time capsule containing a statement drawn up by Arthur Whitworth, the first Clerk to the Council.

Foulridge Parish Council has played an integral part in the life of the village for more than a hundred years. The first Parish Meeting was held on December 4th 1894 when 120 electors met to elect a Parish Council. Originally there were 11 Parish Councillors from all walks of life including a school master, farmer, weaver, draper, coachman, overlooker and solicitor.

Minute book entries vividly reconstruct village life in the early 1900s and provide a fascinating insight into prevailing conditions. The Council in those days was responsible for the provision of public utilities including gas, household water supply and local transport. Roads were not surfaced in tarmac as today and the Council received numerous complaints about the poor condition of streets which were muddy in winter and dusty in summer. The Council also organised sanitation and the collection of household waste which was officially termed 'scavenging'. Before the introduction of sewers and flush toilets, the malodorous muck cart would make its halting progress around the village collecting 'night soil' as did ash carts collecting ashes. This work was carried out by Walton Barritt of Warehouse Lane for more than 25 years, originally with a horse and cart, and later with a motor wagon. The Barritts ceased to collect during the Second World War and Burnley RDC took over the job, suggesting that householders convert from ashpits to dustbins.

The early history of **the Village Hall** is closely linked to that of Foulridge Ambulance Division which raised the money to purchase the land on Town Gate on which the hall was built.

Originally known as the Assembly Hall, the building was completed with the help of a donation from Edward Carr, who was a generous benefactor to the village. The Parish Council, which had been meeting in the National school, was given the use of the hall, accepted trusteeship and made arrangements to heat the building 'by means of steam from the New Shed'. The Deed to the Assembly Hall records that '*if at any time in the future the membership of the Ambulance Association should fall below six the property should pass entirely to the Parish Council as a Village Hall*'. This actually occurred in the late 1950s. A **Village Hall Committee** was formed in 1959 to ensure the smooth running of the place and help organize events and lettings. When the Committee celebrated its 30th anniversary the chief guest was Mrs Evelyn Hargreaves of Town Gate who was the only person remaining on the committee when it was formed.

The village was lighted by 36 lamps presented by Edward Carr. Until the conversion of **street lighting** from gas to electricity in 1953 the Parish Council was responsible for the appointment of a lamplighter. An entry in 1895 records

Water shortage, Town Gate c1930.

that lamps were lighted on the high road to Kirk Bridge '*in the early morning soon after 5 o'clock for the convenience of work people passing along the road*'. James Hartley was appointed lamplighter at a salary for the winter term of £5. The lamps were to be lit every night 'except clearly moonlight nights'. The commencement time for extinction was 10.00 p.m. on week nights, 10.30 on Saturdays.

A main preoccupation of early Parish Council meetings was the provision of a **household water supply** and various schemes utilising Low Well water were considered. One suggestion was for a windmill as motive power for raising the water, but this was deemed somewhat precarious and unsatisfactory. Another proposal was the construction of a reservoir at Moorlands to store the water from nearby springs.

For several hundred years wells and springs provided villages with water. **Kit Syke** provided water for washing for the people of Town Top, whilst drinking water came from **Trent Well**, higher up Trent Lane. The main source of water for the lower part of the village came from **Low Well** which was never known

The Bold Venture Fire Engine outside the Hare & Hounds in the early 1900s. The old horse-drawn engine came into service in 1886 but it was not until 1908 that Foulridge accepted Colne's offer of the use of the engine.

Jack Tom Smith, better known as 'J T' was a major figure in the village for many years. He served as a medical orderly in both Boer and First World Wars, and later was Superintendent of the Foulridge St John Ambulance Division for over 40 years. He was Clerk to the Parish Council for 28 years (1926-1954).

to dry up even in the severest of summer droughts. Even after the introduction of the gravity fed piped water supply from the reservoir at Whitemoor, villagers had to regularly revert to the old stone trough on Town Gate each summer when the level of the reservoir invariably lowered and reduced the supply to a trickle. During water shortages the **well at Burwains** was used to supplement Low Well supplying water to people in the Waller Hill area. After serving the village so well for so long, the flow of water to Low Well gradually eased off in the 1950s until it disappeared altogether.

The Parish Council was also responsible for **fire protection**, and in 1908 entered an agreement with Colne Town Council whereby the village paid the sum of £10 per annum for the services of the Colne Fire Brigade.

The Last Will and Testament of James Baldwin of Accrington provides some interesting background on one of Foulridge's benefactors and the originator of **Baldwin's Charity**. James Baldwin died in 1915 leaving £400, the annual interest to be paid to the people of the village, who, in the opinion of the Parish Council, were 'the most needy or deserving'.

Who was James Baldwin? He was born in Foulridge in 1853, one of seven children of Thomas Baldwin who kept a grocer's shop. Although he moved to Accrington in later life he evidently retained a 'soft spot' for his native village. He always came, like many old Folriggers, on Rushbearing Sunday. He was handicapped with lameness but worked hard, had a good business head, made money and in the end left it to help others whom he felt might need a little extra.

In the early days distribution took the form of clogs, clothes and 'eatables', but from about 1930 it was made in cash. The total income distributed was never more than £20 but many years ago grateful folk received £1 for a long period until they died. With inflation the gift today is very small but the Parish Council is still obliged to pay it out each year. In recent years the Mayor of Pendle has presented the money at the annual Christmas Party for Senior Citizens to the oldest man, woman and longest married couple in the village who were actually present.

The work of the Parish Council has changed over the years and a number of its duties have been taken over by the Borough or the County Council. Nevertheless it fulfils an important role in championing the quality of village life and being the first point of contact for villagers with concerns on current issues within the village and its surroundings. It is a non-political body and liaises with Pendle Borough Council, Lancashire County Council, Lancashire Constabulary, the Fire Service, the NHS Trust and North West Ambulances to ensure that Foulridge receives a proper level of public services. The Council's duties today include receiving planning applications and making recommendations to Pendle Council, letting out allotments, grazing land and sports fields, maintaining roadside verges and wayside seats, and Councillors retain an interest in footpaths, bridleways and traffic issues. The Council has kept pace with the times and is proactive. It has an excellent website which is regularly updated – **www.foulridgeparishcouncil.co.uk**

In 1994 the Parish Council celebrated its centenary. To mark the celebration a number of events were organised ranging from guided walks, a Fun Day and Morris Dancing on the village green. To celebrate the Millennium the Council reinstated a water supply to Low Well.

Low Well Millennium Plaque.

Foulridge Parish Council 2010, from left to right:
Andrew Wilson (Chairman), Rob Oldland, Betty Taylor (Clerk), Graham Cannon, Ruth Sutton, Chris Hobson, Carol Belshaw, Neil Barker.

Foulridge Parish Council has a **Five Year Plan** of projects aimed at benefitting and enhancing the village. Recent examples of projects include the 'Beating the Bounds' walk and leaflet (2007), the 'Welcome to Foulridge' roadside planters (in 2008) and a current proposal to erect a plaque on the A56 main road to commemorate the fact that the Pennine Watershed runs through the village.

After a break of many years, a group of volunteers known as *Foulridge Fundraisers* have allied themselves with the Parish Council's Village Hall Committee. They have started the annual *Foulridge Funday*. Held in June, this has become an eagerly awaited event in the calendar. A continuous programme of events take place at the Village Hall, and these are all advertised on the Parish Council website.

Below left: The Caretaker of the Village Hall for over 30 years, Mrs Yvonne Dwyer Roberts, recently retired from her post. On 8 February 2010 the Parish Council presented her with a crystal bowl in appreciation of her loyal service. She insisted on remaining as reserve however!

Below: Beating the Bounds leaflet.

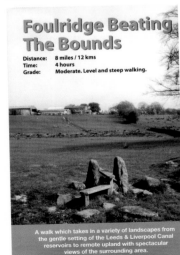

Foulridge Beating The Bounds

Distance: 8 miles / 12 kms
Time: 4 hours
Grade: Moderate. Level and steep walking.

A walk which takes in a variety of landscapes from the gentle setting of the Leeds & Liverpool Canal reservoirs to remote upland with spectacular views of the surrounding area.

Chapter 17

A VILLAGE MISCELLANY

Portrait of Elizabeth Parker by James Cranke. From the Browsholme Hall Collection.

Written records of the village's history date to medieval times. Early chroniclers were mainly civil servants who recorded information for tax purposes such as the Hearth Tax, Window Tax etc. These documents contain interesting information about the village in early times particularly about the principal families, and who was living where and when.

Foulridge is fortunate in having a number of chroniclers who have added to our knowledge of the past – they include diarists, artists, photographers, historians, and in more recent times two Colne District Librarians – Wilfred Spencer and Peter Wightman who did much to popularise local history and generate interest in the subject.

The most prolific local diarist was **Elizabeth Shackleton (nee Parker)** whose diaries survive for the period 1764–1781. Born in 1726, the only daughter of John Parker of Browsholme Hall, near Clitheroe, Elizabeth married her cousin, Robert Parker of Alkincoats. Her Diaries provide a remarkably frank glimpse of life locally in the Georgian era. Elizabeth comments on everything – the progress of the Leeds & Liverpool Canal, the food she ate and the local gentry with whom she socialized. She was blithely unconscious of the cruelty of her age. She attended bull baits at Foulridge and elsewhere, and accepted cockfighting and public flogging as entertainment.

Charles Green (1884–1975)

Charles Green, local historian and photographer

Some of the old photographs used in this book were taken by Charles Green. Born in Barnoldswick in 1884, he moved to Trawden as a small boy and subsequently lived in Foulridge for 70 years.

He started work as a 'half-timer' at the age of 13 as a humble 'raiker-in' or reacher in a weaving mill but, by means of night school study, he achieved both academic and textile qualifications, eventually becoming Managing Director of Hopkinsons (Foulridge) Ltd, New Shed. His leisure time was completely taken up by photography and historical research.

Thomas Robinson (1910–1973)

Born and bred in Foulridge, Thomas Robinson left the village in 1954 to open a grocer's shop in Brierfield, but he remained fascinated by the tales he used to hear from old 'Folriggers' and continued to give illustrated lectures on the history of the village. His photographs, some of which are used in this book, depict buildings, people and events from the 1930s onwards.

Jack Whitaker

Jack Whitaker was related to the Whitaker family who farmed Breeze House in the early 20th century. A builder by trade, writer by inclination, he was the village correspondent from 1935 until the outbreak of war for local newspapers then covering Foulridge. A scrapbook of his press cuttings turned up unexpectedly in the village in 1984, and made interesting reading with headlines such as 'Ram charges and injures pedestrian'. In those days payment was gauged on the number of inches written (6d per inch) – which is why Mr Whitaker kept such accurate records of his work!

Although he ceased to be a journalist, Mr Whitaker remained a wordsmith. A Past President of the Colne Writers' Circle, he won several prestigious awards for his literary talents at the Luther Greenwood Memorial Festival. In 1995 he had a poem published in Poet's England.

Peter Wightman.

Peter Wightman (1933–2001)

Did you know there was once a time when the local tax bill for the whole of Foulridge was £1 6s 8d? Or that mysterious heavenly music was once heard in the parish church – while the building was empty and the organ locked? Or that the first car to crash into Burwains Res was a Ford five-seater tourer in 1912 carrying two Colne piano tuners?

The first burial at Foulridge church was a Kelbrook pauper known as old Shawn. He was knocked down by a horse-drawn charabanc near the garage; Dr Dickey came on horseback to render what assistance he could.

These wonderful stories and more were put together in the early 1980s from various sources by Peter Wightman, former librarian of Colne and Pendle under the title 'Facets of Foulridge'.

Famous Foulridge Fires

The fire at Accornlee on 31 July 1928 is one of the most destructive fires to have occurred in the district. It was caused by newly gathered hay 'sweating' and spontaneously igniting. The photograph shows crowds congregating to watch the fire engulfing the farm buildings bordering on Skipton New Road.

Below left: Weston's fire in the early 1950s

Below right: Accornlee Farm Fire 31 July 1928

The Coronation of Queen Elizabeth II, 2 June 1953

This photograph was taken on the Chapel Steps leading to Town Gate.

Village celebrations took the form of a Fancy Dress Competition with refreshments in the Sunday School. Note the dearth of teenage lads because they considered themselves too grown up to get dressed up!

Christine Bank (Hodges at the time) identified 70 of the 90 on the photograph and various village folk have subsequently supplied further names. We would be pleased to learn the identities of those remaining.

1. John Metcalfe
2. Mrs Pickles
3. P.C. Fred Eccles
4. Len Rushton
5. Wilfred Lee & son Philip
6. Ella Bleasdale
7. Hartley Wilson
8.
9. Mr Thorpe (Malcolm's dad)
10. Mrs Thorpe
11. Margaret Metcalfe (nee Crabtree)
12. Mrs Olga Pickles
13 Kevin Pickles
14. Ken Pickles
15. Kathleen Proctor ?
16. Edward Bleasdale
17. Mrs Bleasdale
18. Lily Pickles / Millie Sutton ?
19.
20 Colin Wilkinson
21. Kathleen Aggus
22. Peter Thornton ?
23. Claire Barrett
24. Anne Thornton
25. Mrs Dyson (Pamela's mother)
26. Freda Pickles
27. Doreen Ward
28. Mrs Howarth (Jennifer's mother)
29. Malcolm Thorpe
30. Alice Heyworth
31.
32. Donald Greenwood
33. John Kenyon
34. Moira Cox
35. Enid Hargreaves
36. S Greenwood
37. Stuart Banks
38. Jean Heyworth

39. Vicky (Helen Victoria) Hargreaves
40. John Durham
41. Sandra Howarth
42. Carol Metters
43.
44. Valerie Proctor
45. Mary Sutcliffe
46. Ruth Richmond
47. Rosalind Banks
48. Diane Lane
49. Carol Wilkinson
50. Christine Hodges
51. Janet Atkins
52. Sheila Morgan
53. Kathleen Teal
54. Veronica Rushton
55. Audrey Bleasdale
56. Pat Morgan
57. Pat Bleasdale

58. Audrey Leah
59. Pamela Hodges
60.
61. Malcolm? Bancroft
62. ? Bancroft
63. Michael Fothergill
64.
65. Pamela Dyson
66. Maureen Bancroft
67. Barry Fothergill
68. Rosemary Wilson
69.
70. Jacqueline Pemberton
71.
72. David Rushton
73.
74. Irene Wallbank
75.
76. Glenys Starford

77. Gerry Durham
78. Andy Durham
79. John Regan
80. Janet Banks
81. Jack Clark
82. Granton Burrows
83.
84.
85. Jennifer Howarth
86. Wendy Metters
87.
88. Lynne Metters
89.
90. Janet Regan (Elizabeth?)

Page from Foulridge Church Magazine, 1931 illustrates quite vividly that the village was far more self sufficient than today.

The petrol station and garage on Skipton Road, August 1930 when it was owned by Billy Butler. Although the garage changed hands a few times before making way for the Massala Room, it is still referred to as Metcalfes Garage. John and Raymond Metcalfe bought the garage in 1959, when it was still just the two wooden huts and ran the garage for more than thirty years.

The water supply from the reservoir on Whitemoor was inadequate in summer and periods of drought, and the Colne Fire Brigade had to take portable trailer pumps along the canal tow path to a point opposite Accornlee and the water was pumped from the canal – carefully measured and monitored by Dick Draper, but too late to save the barn which was now roofless and totally gutted. The fire caused devastating damage apparently worth more than £1,000 and destroyed the 1611 date stone.

Village Life in the early 20th century

A hundred years ago Foulridge was a bustling village providing both employment and all essential needs. In 1927 there were four shops in Abner Row alone

Despite the Depression of the 1930s which caused much hardship locally including the closure of Haslam's Mill at Colne Waterside, one of the area's main employers, village life continued. It celebrated the Silver Jubilee of George V and, for the Coronation of George VI in 1937 there were fireworks and bunting, and all children up to the age of 14 were given mugs and medals. Prior to the outbreak of World War II Foulridge had three working cotton mills, a bank, building society, post office, garage, blacksmith, joiners and undertakers, and no fewer than twenty shops!

In 1937 the parade of shops on Skipton Road were occupied by the Post Office, run by Mrs Elizabeth Spencer, Martin's Bank which had started life as the Craven Bank at the bottom of Stoney Lane, John Hook the butcher, who also had his own slaughter house 'up Waller Hill', the chip shop run by Dick Banks and at the end of the block was of course Greenwood's Confectionery Shop.

On the other side of Causeway was the cottage occupied by Henry Banks, cobbler and clogger. The top of Causeway was known affectionately as the Monkey Rack, the Hyde Park Corner of Foulridge where villagers would pass the time of day and put the world to rights.

On the opposite side of the main road was the Co-op and Bulcock's hardware store at the end of Belmont. Willie and Mat Bulcock also ran the village smithy at the back of the Hare & Hounds until the 1950s.

As well as the shops on Skipton Road, Station Road and Abner Row there was a fish and chip shop run by Elizabeth Moorhouse across from the Hole in the Wall on Town Gate, a barbers (in a hut at the bottom of Cat Fold ginnel) and a variety of sweetshops, newsagents and grocers. Arthur Birch and Ezra Hartley provided joinery and undertaking services.

The Post Office

Over the years Foulridge Post Office was variously sited. In 1879 it was located on Skipton Road, at the bottom of Ivegate, in premises which later became the village Co-op. By 1911 it had moved to 1 Parkinson Street on Town Gate, but within a decade it was back on the main road at No. 10 Skipton Road with Mrs Elizabeth Spencer the postmistress. When Charles Spencer retired as Headmaster he became the postmaster; the couple were succeeded by their daughters Bessie and Dorothy. In all the Spencer family ran the Post Office for fifty years.

Ronnie Moore, who ran the shop on Parkinson Street at the beginning of the 1970s, bought the PO business when the Spencer sisters retired.

The last village postmasters were Stephen and Christine Letch, landlords of the Hole of the Wall, who desperately tried to keep post office services in Foulridge, initially operating the post office in the pub, and finally from their home in Causeway. Efforts to save the village post office fell on deaf ears and its closure in 2008 was part of a nationwide programme which saw 2,500 branches across the country close.

Tom Hodges shop, Station Road. This photograph was taken directly after refurbishment in the early 1950s which transformed the old fashioned shop to the state of the art at the time! Geoff & June Steele ran the shop from 1965-1989, when they sold the business to George & Susan Baldwin

Below left: Article from the Colne Times, 1 March 1996.

Below right: The Post Office in Parkinson Street. Barbara Bradbury was the postmistress from 1991 until retirement in 2003.

LAST POST FOR MAIL MAN ARTHUR

FOULRIDGE'S very own Postman Pat has delivered his last letter after making sure the villagers got their post on time for the last 45 years.

Mr Arthur Hargreaves was determined to keep posting until he reached his golden milestone of 50 years, but unfortunately he has had to take medical retirement after being a postman for 47 years and seven months.

The popular village postie came to Pendle as an evacuee from Bradford. After the war, when his mother, sister and two brothers returned to their native Yorkshire, he was enjoying his job as so much that he decided to stay.

He started as a boy in 1948 riding the telegram bike. After his two years' National Service, he took to delivering letters on foot in Foulridge, before driving the village post van.

The Millennium

In 2000, as part of the celebrations to commemorate the new Millennium, village butcher and keen photographer David Ingham captured images of every aspect of village life as his record of how things were at that time.

• **David Ingham & son, David Jnr, with Brenda Davies (above)**
Inghams have been the village butchers for almost 40 years, since 1973.

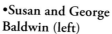

• **PC David Burrows (right)**
A towering personality, nearer seven feet than six feet tall in his police uniform, Dave Burrows was the village bobby from 1979 pounding his rural beat which covered Foulridge and part of Laneshawbridge. He was involved in Scouting in Foulridge including Sea Scouts and, unusually Venture Sea Scouts.

•**Susan and George Baldwin (left)**
The last people to run the newsagents and grocery shop on Station Road.

Girls' Football Team.

Foulridge Youth Team.

Foulridge Minors.

Post Mistress Barbara Bradbury.

Dennis Speak and Trevor Turner.

Ted Dixon's Garage.

Above: The Wood Hut.

Above right: Lakeside Garden Centre.

• Lakeside Garden Centre

The business established in 1973 closed its doors in April 2008 when Mary Ellis, who had run the business for 18 years, retired and sold the land to Howard Rigg of the Manor House.

Other photographs have been included elsewhere, but readers wishing to view the entire time capsule are recommended to log onto the Foulridge Parish Council website to view the full collection. It is surprising how much has changed in the short space of ten years and clearly demonstrates that the story of Foulridge is **a never ending story**.

BIBLIOGRAPHY

Badgery Collection, Lancashire Record Office DDBd

Baines, Edward *History of Lancashire III Vol II, 1870*

Bank, John *The Bank Estate in Foulridge.* 2002

Bannister, Fred *The Annals of Trawden Forest.* Colne & Nelson Times. 1922

Barcroft Manuscripts Parker Muniments, Lancashire Record Office.

Barcroft, Rev John Pim *Barcroft of Barcroft,* 1960

Barrett, William Henry *Whitemoor families* c.1990

Barrett's Directories of Burnley & District, 1879-1949

Byrne, Clifford *Survey of Wayside Crosses in North East Lancashire.* 1978

Carr, James *Annals and Stories of Colne and Neighbourhood, 1st edition 1876 and 2nd edition 1878*

Census Returns 1851, 1881, 1901

Colne Parish Registers *Baptisms & Burials 1599–1812, Marriages 1599–1837*

Colne & Nelson Times 1874–

Cross, Ralph Transcriptions of the Diaries of Elizabeth Shackleton (1764-1781) Colne Library

Crowther, Doreen Family Pedigrees and Digest of local property deeds, 1980s. Colne Library

Cryer, Mrs *Memories of Colne.* Colne & Nelson Times 1910

Dalby, Allan Transcriptions of the Elizabeth Shackleton Diaries. Colne Library

Ekwall, Eilert *Placenames of Lancashire* 1922

Oxford Dictionary of English Place-names 1960

English Heritage *Pendle Textile Mills,* Architectural Survey Report. 2000

Farrer, W *Court Rolls of the Honor of Clitheroe, Vols 1 & 2 1377–1567.* 1897

Foulds, T *Old Roads of Colne* n.d.

Foulridge Methodist Chapel Souvenir 1872-1972 Centenary services

France, R Sharpe, MA *A High Constable's Register* 1681. Reprinted from the Transactions of the Historic Society of Lancashire & Cheshire Vol. 107, 1955

Jessop *Account of Methodism in Rossendale 1880*

Mannex *Trade Directory,* 1854

Marquis, James T *Some Local Crosses.* Barrowford Almanac 1912

Nuttall, Barbara H *A History of Thornhill,* 1963

Oldland, Fay *Foulridge History Trail.* Pendle Civic Trust. 1981

   Felt Hatting in Foulridge and Colne. Pendle Heritage Centre 1981.

   Foulridge Past & Present. Colne Library. 1984

   Story of Foulridge. Pendle Heritage Centre. 1990

Robinson, Thomas Tape recordings. Colne Library.

Sephton, John *A Handbook of Lancashire Place-names.* 1913

Shackleton, Elizabeth *Diaries* (1764–81). Lancashire Record Office

Shackleton, Geoff *The Textile Mills of Pendle and their Steam Engines.* Landmark. 2006

Shackleton, Pamela *The Birth of a New Church* (Foulridge 1905). 1982

Smith, Phil *Haunting of Hobstones.* Pendle District Libraries Local History Notes No. 7

Spencer, Wilfred M *Colne As It Was.* Hendon Publishing. 1971

   Another Look at Colne. Colne Parish Register Transcriptions. 1972

Spencer, Wilfred M (Ed) *Memorandum Book of Ambrose Barcroft* (1689–1693) and
   Account Book of Thomas Barcroft (1693–1732)

Taft, Mary *Memoirs.* 1817

Taylor, Henry *The Ancient Crosses of Lancashire.* Reprinted from the Transactions of the Lancashire & Cheshire Antiquarian Society Vol. XVIII. 1901

Ten Broeck Runk, Emma *Barcroft Family Records.* An account of the family in England and descendants of Ambrose Barcroft, Pennsylvania. 1910

Thompson, Edwin *This Remarkable Family. A study of the Barritts of Foulridge 1750–1850.* 1981

Victoria County History *A History of Lancashire, Volume 6.* 1911

Whitaker, T D *A History of Whalley and the Honor of Clitheroe,* 4th edition, Volumes I & II, 1872

Whitttaker, Gladys *The Loss of the Piedmont 1795.* Pendle Heritage Centre 1981

Wightman, Peter *Bonnie Colne.* Hendon Publishing 1975

   Facets of Foulridge. Unpublished. Colne Library 1981

INDEX